GET OUT OF I.T. WHILE YOU CAN.

GET OUT OF I.T. WHILE YOU CAN.

A GUIDE TO EXCELLENCE FOR PEOPLE IN I.T.

Craig Schiefelbein

iUniverse, Inc.

New York Lincoln Shanghai

Get Out of I.T. While You Can.
A Guide to Excellence for People in I.T.

iUniverse books may be ordered through booksellers or by contacting:

iUniverse
2021 Pine Lake Road, Suite 100
Lincoln, NE 68512
www.iuniverse.com
1-800-Authors (1-800-288-4677)

The views expressed in this work are solely those of the author and do not necessarily reflect the views of the publisher, and the publisher hereby disclaims any responsibility for them.

ISBN-13: 978-0-595-41357-7 (pbk)
ISBN-13: 978-0-595-85724-1 (cloth)
ISBN-10: 0-595-41357-9 (pbk)
ISBN-10: 0-595-85724-8 (cloth)

Printed in the United States of America

Praise for *Get Out of IT*

"Getting out of IT and into your industry is what it takes to be great in IT. Great message!"
Mark Henderson, Section Head Technical Support Services, Mayo Clinic

"Craig's message inspires all employees to realize their role in driving organizational success. A must-hear message for all!"
Betty Barhorst, President, Madison Area Technical College

"Getting out of IT and into your industry is the catalyst for innovation that drives real business value."
Carl Christiansen, CIO, Marshfield Clinic

This simple message eludes many in this world. Our job is to support the business—if people don't get this, success is impossible.
Mike Jones, CIO, Children's Hospital

"Craig's message is universal. Anyone in any department (not just IT) can benefit from this message. And it applies to private sector and public sectors equally. The more we understand Craig's message in the public sector, the more we can focus on the true business of government."
Matt Miszewski, CIO, State of Wisconsin

"Everyone in IT can benefit from this message. It will get them, their IT organization, their company and the real customer to a better place."
Judy Murphy, Vice President Information Services, Aurora Healthcare

"Craig's book is really about leadership. He articulates a key thought process that drives great leaders at all levels of successful organizations."
Dirk Debbink, President, MSI General

Contents

Preface

When the marketing department at my company, PDS, heard that I began writing a book, it took about two days for the local media to publish articles about my project. Although I appreciated that the marketing team was good at public relations, I wasn't sure if I wanted anyone to know. This would be my first book, and who knew how long it would take to write? Secondly, who knew if it would be any good?

Following my early press coverage, I would run into people (or get phone calls) and get a series of questions:

Hey, I saw you are writing a book. Are you going to tell your story?
No, the book isn't about me.

Is it about PDS?
No, it doesn't have to do with me or PDS.

What is it about, then?
It is about getting people to a better place in their career and life. It is aimed primarily at anyone who works within an IT organization (which some call computer department, information services, IT, hardware support, software development … you name it).

So it's about technology?
Nope. It has little to do with technology. In fact, the book could have been named *Get Out of HR, Finance, Administration,* etc. The bottom line is that over the last twenty years, I have been watching good people, who have good intentions and work ethic, fail to understand their value. I believe I can help.

Oh. So it's a career growth book?

Yes, and hopefully more. Quality of life, confidence, and opportunity (even compensation) can increase when one is more respected within their job. At work, respect comes as one strives to add real business value. It is hard for a person to add business value without understanding the purpose, strategy, and competitive landscape of their employer. If I can simplify how one can see these variables, they will benefit. Furthermore, if I can help some individuals see their role in innovating to help their organization compete, that's even better. Finally, if they can see their role in mentoring others and fostering a culture of innovation and agility … well, that's the ultimate state to be in.

Sounds good. I didn't know you were a writer.

I don't know if I am. I just know that I have a purposeful message that can help people get to a better place. Why not share it? Believe me, I have no illusions of winning a Pulitzer Prize—only making the world a little better. I know that I am just a simple man trying to get into heaven.

Acknowledgments

I would like to thank all of my customers and colleagues over the years. Much of what I know comes from watching them do great things. It is hard to list everyone, but you know who you are.

For the purposes of this book, clients that I received input from include Carl Christensen (CIO, Marshfield Clinic), Reid Engstrom (Director of Technical Services Harley-Davidson Motor Company), Chuck Heiting (Administration and Planning Manager, Marshfield Clinic), Mark Henderson (Section Head, Microcomputer Technology, Mayo Clinic), Steve Jaeger (VP of Information Services and Infrastructure, Quad/graphics), Mike Jones (CIO, Children's Hospital of Wisconsin), Dennis Kuester (CEO and Chairman, M&I Bank), Keith Livingston (CIO, Thedacare), Matt Miszewski, (CIO, State of Wisconsin), Jerry Roberts (CIO, Dean Healthcare), Rick Roy (CITO, Cuna Mutual Group), and Greg Smith (CIO and Senior VP, Wheaton Healthcare).

Many colleagues provided support and perspective through the writing process, most notably Lance Berg, Maribeth Bush, Dirk Debbink, Mike Grall, Gareth Harwood, Chris Liburdi, Kerry Marti, Tom Mount, Todd Radke, and Carl Wilhelm.

This being my first major writing project, I was very appreciative of proofreading and editing suggestions from Bonnie Hearn-Hill and Todd Radke. Illustrations and moral support came from Gareth Harwood.

Finally, I have to thank my mom for teaching me to issue love, trust, and respect first, and know that everything else would follow; my in-laws for humor and support when needed; and my wife Mary for giving me space to kick out my message.

I would like to thank those who allowed me to reference them:

- Thornton May and CIO Decisions (CIO Habitat Research)
- Ann Vertel, MA, CPBA Marketing and Business Development Coach
- Creative Commons (Innovation Quote)
- Frank J Anderson Jr., Christopher R. Hardy,Ph.D, Chief Learning Officer Magazine (Agile Learning)
- Paige Leavitt and American Productivity & Quality Center (Rewarding Innovation)

Introduction

Over the last twenty years, I have been blessed to work with many great individuals within my company—Paragon Development Systems, Inc. (PDS)—and many great individuals within our clients' information technology (IT) departments. This client list includes companies like Alliant Energy, Children's Hospital, CUNA Mutual, Froederdt Hospital, Harley-Davidson, Kohl's, M&I Bank, Marshfield Clinic, Mayo Clinic, Quadgraphics, WE Energies, Wheaton Healthcare, and quite a few more. Many have shared with me the lessons they have learned in order to accomplish a common objective: to help a strong population of individuals in IT get to a place where they are adding more value to their employers and getting more respect, confidence, and opportunities.

Many IT professionals today devote 100 percent of their attention to their end-users' uptime, support, and satisfaction. While this is and will always be important, failure to see beyond the "end-user customer" to their "employer's customer" can create real problems. Individuals in IT who are not delivering real business value are increasingly seen as a commodity. Commodity services are bought on price or are outsourced. While I disagree that these services *done well* are commodity, perception is the buyer's reality. This reality can create poor job satisfaction for some in IT; as well as poor job security.

Conversely, those who gain the most respect and get the most opportunities understand their employer's business strategy and purpose. This knowledge creates a mindset change that can help deliver more business value and innovation. Even very small innovations can be extremely valuable. Individuals who see the bigger picture tend to function a little differently. They have an easier time prioritizing tasks that matter most. They are trying to answer questions like, How can I help my employer compete in an increasingly difficult market? How can I drive better client experience or create more loyal customers? Is there something I can do to help capture more market share or drive the business strategy?

So that's it! After working with hundreds of information technology organizations (ITOs) and thousands of IT professionals, I found that the common denominator among the great ones is that they do not see themselves as being "*in* IT." Instead, they see themselves in the same business as their employer, be it medicine or motorcycles. That is to say that the term *IT Professional* should only be used if one's employer's invoices are filled with IT products and services. Otherwise, to lead effectively, they see themselves as serving the needs of healthcare, banking, education, government service, manufacturing, utilities, etc. I am not saying that one shouldn't celebrate being a technical guru, but you should choose to be the best in your industry. A good leader might not see this as unique. Unfortunately, my experience has shown me that many in IT don't understand this concept.

Get Out of IT While You Can has two meanings. First, individuals need to get out of IT "while they can" to understand the purpose, strategy, and industry of their employers. This book is filled with useful exercises and anecdotes to help facilitate this; I believe working through these is the first step that will lead to many benefits, including a better quality of life.

The second meaning of "while you can" refers to the ITO as a whole. Most organizations in our global marketplace exist in a low-margin, hard-to-sustain position. If most members of an IT department do not clearly understand their business strategy, or their employer's industry, they will fail to attain or maintain market leadership.

Seeing yourself as part of the larger picture, and not simply in IT, could transform your career and possibly save it. In this book, you are going to learn how to do just that.

Chapter One

The Best You Can Be Is Not Enough

The Best You!

You cannot have what you want if you are content to remain what you are.

—Robin Sharma

Chapter One: The Best You Can Be Is Not Enough!

It is no longer good enough to choose to be the best you—
you have to choose to be the best you in your industry.

As the CEO of a $100 million IT solutions company, I am blessed to have great relationships with many people inside IT organizations. My position also gives me the privilege of having strong relationships with executive management outside of IT. This gives me a unique perspective that occasionally brings to light differing perceptions of priorities and charters. Like all businesses, ours is about providing value to the client organization. In IT, business value is tied purely to its alignment to the business purpose and strategy. So how do purpose and strategy get lost so often in IT?

The Story Begins …

I was having a conversation about work and life with a veteran IT professional I have known for many years. This person, whom I will call Charlie, was a great guy. Charlie was a hard worker with a good sense of humor. Like many who work within IT departments, Charlie prided himself on his happy computer users. He was also committed to personal growth.

Like many people in IT, he started his career in IT. He had an interest in computers and got a job as a break/fix technician. His work ethic and service were great; customers liked him. He took ownership of whatever task was before him, even if it required late nights and weekends. This level of commitment got him promoted regularly over time. First he was promoted to oversee all the break/fix technicians. Then, in addition, he was given a leadership roll over the Help Desk.

Charlie, self-driven for success, would study regularly so he could gain more technical expertise. In time, he obtained his computer network engineering certifications (MCSE and CNE). Then, beyond managing technicians and a help desk, Charlie found himself on the Network Infrastructure Committee. Before too long, Charlie was promoted to oversee the entire IT organization for his company. His drive and work ethic got him promoted to IT director of a $50+ million services company where there wasn't a CIO. Well done, Charlie!

He was extremely happy with his advancement. His career had great momentum, and he didn't want it to stop. Being self-driven, he wanted further growth and opportunity as a leader in his company. Whereas some people have a hard time choosing between being loved and respected, he did not. He wanted to be respected as a real contributor. Charlie's new long-term goal was to be on his company's board of directors one day. He shared this with executive management and found that they were not closed to the idea. However, they first needed Charlie and his IT department to "become more of a strategic partner to the organization". Charlie wasn't clear on what this meant exactly, but with his hard work, he would figure it out.

Charlie continued to work hard, but over time, something happened. Charlie felt his respect and advancement stagnate. Charlie's perspective became that executive management didn't see how hard he was working or how complex IT could be. He started to become a little disenchanted.

From Charlie's perspective, there was a gap between his role in the company and how he wanted to be perceived by management (as a business leader). From management's perspective, there was a gap between Charlie's understanding of his job (providing what they thought were utility services) and how they needed him to contribute (as a business leader). The gap was obvious from the outside, but not easily grasped by my friend in IT.

From management's perspective, the real value of IT had little to do with performing *utility* aspects (uptime, security, technology refresh and support). Utilities are supposed to always be on, and tend to be taken for granted. Executive management, as in most businesses today, was looking for someone with technical skills who would take an interest in their business. They wanted someone to understand their purpose, customer demand, trends, competitive landscape, and their position in that landscape. A real contributor could be an entry-level IT person who took up this business interest and offered even small suggestions regarding how they could improve their business position.

Executive management wanted and needed for Charlie to see the bigger picture. They even insisted that he attend sales and operations management meetings. By doing so, perhaps he could begin to understand what their customers go through in a day. Their hope was that he could apply IT to drive their strategy. Charlie complied, and why not? Being perceived as a utility or commodity certainly wasn't the way to job satisfaction.

Management was hopeful that Charlie's work ethic and aptitude would help him to see the business needs as he attended these meetings. If he could, Charlie might inspire them with fresh ideas. *Management wanted to be inspired by IT leadership on how IT could be applied to improve its customers' experiences, decisional data, market share, drive efficiencies, and so forth.* Their measures for success were spelled out clearly in their strategic plan. Hadn't Charlie heard that the business value of IT is in direct proportion to its alignment with the strategic plan? Go, Charlie, go!

Being driven to succeed, Charlie always went to his sales and operational meetings well prepared with a list of all the projects the IT team was working on. In his mind, the meetings would be successful if everyone could see how hard they were working and that they were doing a good job. Management's idea was failing. Being in *send mode* instead of *receive mode*, he wasn't listening well to the day in the life of the company's customer. Charlie wasn't thinking about how IT could add value to their offerings (or coming up with new ones). He wasn't looking to drive experiences and efficiencies or eliminate waste. Management's attempt and Charlie's work ethic failed to bridge the gap. Both sides were frustrated.

My heart went out to Charlie. I also felt management's frustration. Could I help bridge the gap? The gap was glaringly evident to me. Perhaps I could mentor my friend a little. I have seen so many in IT break through from tactical to strategic thinking over the years. It doesn't have to be hard at all. Open the mind a little, throw in some time and light bulbs will start going on.

I asked Charlie some IT business questions to get his perspective:

> *Of all of the IT services you provide, which are most important to driving the business?*
> *Ummm, I don't know.*

What are you currently working on in IT to enhance your
company's customer experience or improve product offerings?
I would have to think on that one for a while.

If you were selling your IT services externally, what would
your company's competitor buy from you?
Ummm, I don't know.

I ask, Charlie, because I want to know if you have a focus on
issues that are meaningful to your business. Let me ask you,
who do you see as the market leader in your industry?
I'm not really sure.

Therefore I had to skip the next question.—Well, then, how
are the market leaders applying IT to drive business value?
No answer.

Can you tell me who your competition is?
After a long pause, Charlie responded with a light list and in
a questioning tone of voice.

Then, finally, it came out! It was a response that can be either wonderful or crippling depending on a number of factors. Here was the response that got him far, but not far enough. The response:

"I just choose to be the best me I can be."

In this case, I did and do completely believe that he *chooses to be the best him* each day when he gets up. It is a great choice and my hope is that you, the reader are already this far. This great level of self-motivation puts him ahead of the curve. However, without understanding his company's purpose, strategy, and industry, his value to the company was limited.

I let Charlie know that choosing to be the best person you can be is no longer enough if you want to be seen as a real player in the business. It certainly is a virtuous choice and makes for good organizational morale. However, an individual could work for their entire career without adding any discernable business value to their employer. Someone with great work ethic and intent might never suggest how they might do something a little different to improve their clients' experiences, employer's market share, competitive position, or real productivity, etc. Instead, they focus only on diminishing down time, increasing bandwidth, and improving user satisfaction. Charlie, I said, don't be the best you can be, but *the best you in your employer's industry.*

Furthermore, I shared that the only IT individuals who make it to the board level or have the respect of business and board leaders don't see themselves as being "in IT," but as being in the same industry that their employers'. They make a conscious decision to internalize their company's business strategy. They allocate time to understand their organization's clients, not just the users they are supporting.

The people in IT who really contribute to their organizations, competitively analyze their industry peers. They go online to see how market-leading organizations and individuals are driving value or creating a competitive advantage. They combine lessons learned with industry trends and look for opportunities to improve and innovate. This is one of the differences between management and leadership in IT. They are asking themselves; how can I help drive my employer's strategy?

Please believe that I am not picking on Charlie. This book is dedicated to the many hard-working individuals who get sucked into the quagmire of IT trench warfare and then fail to see the big picture. It is written with sympathy for those who want purpose, security, and opportunity, but can't find it.

> *It is no longer good enough to choose to be the best you—you have to choose to be the best you in your industry!*

As I spoke with Charlie, an observation entered my mind. I knew he was very competitive in all other aspects of his life. It didn't matter whether it was sports, departmental competition or Rock, Paper, Scissors; Charlie wanted to win! Yet, he never considered it his job to help his company win in its competitive landscape. Maybe it's the trench warfare mentality that many get in IT? You can find extremely competitive people never helping their employer compete within their industry as a part of their job. What a waste of competitive ingenuity!

One of the obstacles in my friend's way stemmed from his career path. Like many others in IT, he began his career in IT. His education, experiences, and passion were shaped by his time working in IT. He had been seen as a superstar for being "the IT guy" who could solve most technical problems and communicate well at the same time. These are attributes not always found together in great IT engineers.

Quite honestly, it is impressive to earn a spot on the management team of a business without any business training and with limited God-given business acumen. I know many people who have accomplished this feat and have much to be proud of. Great technical prowess and communication skills will consistently get you promoted. Unfortunately, without business savvy or training, these promoted individuals will eventually end up in positions of incompetence. There is no shortage of Peter Principle case studies in ITOs, which is why I am writing this book.

My colleague Michael Grall shared the converse point with me.

> Almost all people graduating from business school have some technical background. As students, they learn how companies are applying technology to get better decisional data, drive better client experiences, or increase geographic trading area. It is also standard practice that business students use current technology. Frequently, they then go to work for a company and wonder why the IT team isn't fully informed of all these business (not technology) case studies.

One result of working in IT without a business education is that business unit leaders are taking away IT sourcing decisions from those in IT. Those in IT who chose vendors yesterday are today competing with vendors for their jobs. The trend of IT sourcing decisions being removed from IT is increasing at a rapid rate. That is scary thought for most of us in IT.

Talk about a loss of control! There are more and more stories about IT staffs that were once celebrated for providing great service and are now fighting for job security. Their business now calls them "tactical". Those who once believed that they were in charge of such decisions now realize that they are not.

We will discuss job protection and sourcing strategies in future chapters. For now, realize that *not* growing into your industry or engaging in trench warfare can be a losing proposition.

> *It is not the mountain we conquer but ourselves.*
> —*Sir Edmund Hillary*

You Don't Understand—I Can't Get Out of IT and into My Business!

These types of career challenges seem daunting. After I challenged Charlie to see his role as greater than just his job in IT, he responded, "If I get out of IT and into my business, who is going to do my job, support my infrastructure and users?"

I sensed fear, confusion, and a combination of defenses from a smart, hard-working guy. I wanted to jump in and show him that it can be easy and fun to get to the desired state. The remainder of the book is the approach to get you there. It is a laymen's approach to career success in IT.

Before I shared things that Charlie should start, stop, or think about doing to be great in IT, I recognized that I needed him to get out of the way of himself. His frustrations with management built up a defense system. For him to really grasp how easy the shift from tactical to strategic thinking was, we had to tear down his wall. His tone of voice and my instinct led me to believe that he had a combination of defenses:

- *You are pie in the sky and don't understand what I do!* He was right; I can't fully understand what he goes through in a day. Understanding his management's viewpoint, I was hoping that he would trust that I was looking out for his best interests.

- *I gave birth to much of what I do. The policies, procedures, toolsets and people I have grown are my babies. I can't leave them.* For this emotion, I am truly sympathetic. The fear of parting with the familiar is understandable. However, I wasn't asking him to leave anything. I was simply suggesting that he might grow to do whatever he wanted, even if it was the same thing.
- *This is foreign to me. Where do I start? Can I make the jump? What if I look stupid for trying?* Both the fear of failure and the fear of looking foolish by asking what felt like naïve business questions were stopping him.

We continued to talk, and Charlie started to realize that his defenses were clouding his judgment. The challenges I laid before him were for him, not to him. We talked through his defenses, and the journey (and this book) began. Charlie and I would get together again soon.

This book is not written solely for those individuals stuck in the trench warfare of IT. It is written for everyone at every level within the IT organization. That is because good individuals and organizations recognize that *leadership must happen at all levels* within your organization. You have a responsibility to help mentor those around you so they can get to their desired state. Before moving on, I want to throw out some food for thought on mentoring,

As you mentor individuals in IT, you might have to get them out of the way of themselves. All of us have to get out of the way of ourselves on occasion. Getting out of IT is not that difficult. Whether you are mentoring someone else or establishing goals for yourself, it is helpful to understand some common reasons why a person can be stuck "in IT" to begin with:

- They experience a fear of failure.
- They have a job-vs.-career mentality.
- They misunderstand or doubt business leadership.
- They believe that moving forward or teaching someone their position is as good as eliminating job security.

Imagine you are writing your autobiography or some else's biography (by mentoring). If you really wanted to write a story of success in life, you'd begin by addressing obstacles and resistors to growth. If you can identify the resistance to your own growth, the lessons in remaining chapters of this book become very simple to apply.

Go through the following list of resistance types and try to understand which ones apply to you. By becoming aware of these factors, you can train your internal dialogue to coach yourself past them. This is maturation in its truest form. Do any of the following types of resistance to change apply? This is your book—feel free to circle applicable ones.

Resistors to Growth (and Possible Solutions)

- *Fear of failure or uncertainty.* How natural and strong. Trust me, it is better to try tactfully and fail than not try. Trying gets respect; worry and complacency do not. Try to identify those who can mentor you and seek their assistance. They will feel respected by your request.

- *Poor mentorship/low educational support.* Ask for support or guidance. If you don't get it where you are, accept responsibility for yourself. There are no shortages of resources available. Research on the Internet, grow your industry-related affiliations, or shadow the job of a customer-facing colleague.

- *IT leadership is "in IT" not "in any given industry."* If you know someone who feels this way; buy them this book!

- *A non-purposeful company.* Most companies serve a human-need purpose, regardless of their industry. Identify it for your company and perpetuate it within your team. If you can't do that, go find a place whose corporate mission speaks to you. You will have a hard time optimizing the quality of your life if there isn't purpose in your career.

- *I am comfortable where I'm at in my job.* I would challenge that you cannot have respect staying that way for the long term. You will be passed up while passing on opportunity. If you don't think you have to compete, you won't.

- *Loss of control/this is my baby.* Keep control! Establish specific, time-bound goals that add business value. However, if you think "This is my baby" means that no one can do it without you, join the billions of people in cemeteries who thought the same thing.

- *Lack of trust with business leadership.* Study the annual report and strategic plans, job shadow, and ask questions. Be noble and offer the olive branch to management first. If you can't establish trust, leave. However, if you have always had an issue with authority figures, think about why and get past it. Your quality of life will always be diminished otherwise.

- *Leadership is weak.* Did you ever consider mentoring the mentor, or the mentor's mentor? The second meaning of *while you can* is that no business is secure without the whole team on board. Take charge!

- *Culture of company.* Bottom-up cultures are great because everyone has a voice. However, the bottom will often hold itself down, defending past decisions. Secondly, if your company's culture makes people feel that they are dependent on the company instead of the other way around, try to change it or leave. Finally, if there is no long-term ownership of initiatives (people move or are reassigned often), projects will fail and financial support will fade.

- *Culture of the IT organization.* The cultures of many IT organizations are built by individuals like the one in this chapter. They celebrate old-school metrics and honor history. Knowledge gained through exercises in this book can help you impact this culture positively.

- *Negative attitude/no future here.* Is there really "no future" there, or do you feel misunderstood? Change perceptions of yourself and your organization or send out resumes.

- *The* "never outsource" *mindset.* Outsourcing doesn't necessarily mean sending work to India, China, or Mexico. Believe it or not, developing a competency in sourcing in this flat world might actually be your security. Pick your battles, choose your allies.

- *Shortage of vendors in immediate area* to perform tactical services. You will be forced to provide economical and efficient support services while innovating in areas of business value. To do this effectively requires more resources than most ITOs get. Recognize that if most of your innovative capacity is being allocated to tactical support areas instead of solutions that drive business value, you will never get the financial support to do both effectively.

- *Any other reason?* Tell me at http://www.getoutofit.net.

Looking at this list with sober self-assessment makes waiting in line at the Department of Motor Vehicles feel like a holiday. However, we often make these obstacles bigger than ourselves. I have seen many IT professionals overcome these challenges through a wide array of actions or personal styles. The one common action is to soberly assess the situation and choose to do something about it. Picture yourself in your desired reality. To get to that place, what needs to occur today? Which of the resistance types need to be dealt with? There insightful illustrations in the next three chapters that will help spark revelation.

Even if all of this seems frightfully common, and you even feel complete in your current role, there is a great reason to defend where you are. By feeling complete, I mean that

- You have purpose.
- Your work charter is clear and relevant.
- You are excelling and respected for it.
- All of your customers (consumers, users and boss) are happy.
- You have balance.

If this is the case, congratulations! Defend it by being wise. Continually educate yourself. Execute and market your successes at work. So many positions in IT are increasingly becoming perceived as commodities, even though they might not be. The best positions in IT today might be ones taken for granted in the future. No one wants to be taken for granted or viewed as a commodity, a metric with cost containment as a primary charter. Education, execution, and marketing can defend against these perceptions.

Again, if you want grow in your current position or into a new one, congratulations! That you are reading this is a great indicator that you care. So this is your career and autobiography. What is your desired state of livelihood or being? What obstacles would you like to overcome? The remainder of the book will help you answer these questions. It is a laymen's approach to career success in IT.

When we talk about leadership later, you should also understand that you should help others get past their points of resistance. Leadership happens at all levels in your organization.

Chapter One: Action Items/Points to Ponder

1) Are you choosing to be the best you everyday? If not, what is preventing you?

_____

_____

_____

2) Of the large list of resistors to growth in this chapter, list the ones you need to get past to reach your potential?

_____

_____

_____

3) How will you get past them (and by when)?

_____

_____

_____

Point to Ponder:

Who is the model to emulate? One objective of this book is to help people reach a deeper level of contentment. Take five minutes to think of someone who represents the "complete package" to you. What of their characteristics do you most admire? How do they deal with adversity? What separates your state of being from their state of being (i.e., business acumen, inner peace, confidence, enthusiasm, innovativeness)? Others identify a role model to engage for life mentoring. Ponder if you can do that for someone, or if you would like that for yourself.

<u>NOTES</u>

NOTES

Purpose

Chapter Two

A man sees two guys digging a ditch. He asks them what they are doing. The first replies, "I am digging a ditch." The second replies, "We are building a hospital."

—Author unknown

Chapter Two: Purpose

I stand with an accomplished IT director who chooses to be the best he can be every day. While his track record and work ethic in IT are great, he has failed to recognize his role in his company's success. After conveying my message to him—that being his best isn't enough if he wants to be recognized as a major contributor—he asked, "To become the best in the industry, where does one need to start?" Although I didn't have a formal mentoring approach, reply came quickly, "Purpose!"

A look of puzzlement crossed his face. I explained that all businesses start and exist because of need. Furthermore, successful companies and workers see beyond their role of providing products or services. Successful companies serve the deeper human needs of their customers. That need could be to feel more confident, respected, appreciated, or even beautiful. Perhaps the customer just wants his day to be less burdensome. Regardless of the niche that they fill, businesses grow when they serve their purpose well. Hence, being the best you in your industry requires that you first recognize the human need, or purpose, that your company and industry serve.

I could see that some light bulbs were going on in his head. Unfortunately our conversation had to end because of other commitments, but we agreed to get together soon and continue the discussion.

As we parted, I recognized that my friend was not alone. I started to ponder why so many of my acquaintances within IT organizations, although happy, seemed to be engaged in a sort of trench warfare. I discussed this with my colleagues Carrie Rhoads and Carl Wilhelm. Together we came up with the idea of engaging the services of an Internet survey company to assess the perceptions of IT workers.

We had the survey company send two questions to 6,083 IT professionals from the industries of banking, healthcare, education, government, and manufacturing. The distribution list was scrubbed to ensure that none of the companies involved in the survey were from the IT industry (meaning their companies did not provide IT products and services). Although none of the companies were from the IT industry, we listed "IT industry" as an option. The first question was "In what industry is your profession?" This litmus test was to see if respondents saw their professions as falling under the heading of IT industry or the industry that provided them their career opportunities. Of those that responded, 54 percent saw themselves as in the IT industry. I was blown away! This became one of a number of catalysts for this book.

To the defense of so many, it is understandable how living within an IT department can pull us away from the forest and into the trees. There is no shortage of projects to address and fires to fight. People do not call when they are happy, but rather when something is wrong. Working in IT also requires a commitment to continuing education that could prompt this response. Maybe it is not necessarily a wrong answer.

There is, however, a better response. My experience with hundreds of IT organizations and thousands of IT professionals is this: those who create the most value, have the most success, and typically enjoy a better quality of life do not see themselves as being in IT, but in the industry and purpose their company serves.

This observation is not mine alone. Many others contributed to the creation of this book. We surveyed key individuals within market-leading organizations, and their feedback was strong and consistently clear. Again, the common denominator was that IT individuals who contributed the most to the success of their organizations did not see themselves as in IT, but in their companies' industry. They served the purposes of healthcare, education, banking, and so forth.

Furthermore, the IT organizations who contributed the most to the success of their companies were those most aligned with the purpose and strategy of that company. In fact, it seemed commonly understood by these individual leaders that market leadership could never be attained/maintained if more than half of the IT organization saw themselves as in IT.

> *Those who create the most value, have the most success, and typically enjoy a better quality of life do not see themselves as in IT, but in the industry and purpose their company serves.*

Quality of Life?

I can honestly say that most of the people I know in IT are generally happy and pleasant to work with. According to the Hudson Employment Index released August 2, 2006, 74 percent of the IT work force was happy with their jobs in July, up from 71 percent in June.

Remember that the survey we sent out had two questions. (The first asked readers to identify their industry of profession). The second question was "How happy are you?" Our overall results resembled the Hudson index with 74 percent responding positively. **However, those who saw themselves in their employer's industry were 22 percent happier than those who saw themselves as in IT.**

It is my hope that the exercises in this book will bring increased happiness to all who attempt them. Furthermore, I would like to see some become whole. I don't believe that happiness and wholeness are the same. Remember the analogy at the beginning of this chapter? The first person ditch digger can be happy, but their potential for wholeness is diminished compared to someone who sees the bigger picture.

Understanding the bigger picture or the greater purpose is the foundation upon which innovative ideas are built. Even a small process innovation can bring huge value if it improves a customer's experience. Those who create such value tend to have more credibility, respect, confidence, inner peace, and compensation.

There is a real opportunity for most people to add more value to their jobs *and* have a better quality of life at the same time by simply working a little smarter or different, though not necessarily harder. It starts with an understanding of purpose.

Seeking Real-Time Purpose

On April 20, 2005, I went to meet Matt Miszewski, the new CIO for the State of Wisconsin. I had met with Matt on a number of occasions and greatly appreciated his perspective and also the challenges he faced. Like many states in the early 2000s, Wisconsin faced serious budget deficits; their 2003 deficit was $3.2 billion. Governor Jim Doyle chartered Matt to find a way to improve government services while reducing the IT budget by $40 million. Matt set out to accomplish both tasks simultaneously.

He began a strong campaign with his leadership team to consolidate all of their tactical aspects of IT. They figured that if they could consolidate much of the state government's ten data centers, 2,500 distributed servers, two dozen help desks and the numerous technology refresh strategies, they could put a huge dent in that $40 million figure. Certainly the risks of consolidation on this scale are great. Wisconsin's distributed infrastructure supports 60,000 users, who in turn support 5.5 million citizens throughout the state.

Beyond the risks of disgruntled users or citizens, you have another type of risk. There are 1,000+ employees within Wisconsin's IT organization. Matt chuckled when I suggested that there is probably some percentage that would like to have him taken out for creating such drastic change.

"I am sure you are right," he said. "However, I see my job as making children healthier, the streets safer, and society more educated. If I can save $8 million on one of my consolidation efforts, I can buy a lot of books." It made me wonder how many of those in IT complaining about the consolidation were also complaining about the support cuts at their children's schools. Which would they choose? He saw his big picture purpose *beyond* providing an always-on, secure, and well-supported infrastructure. He saw his charter not as cost reduction, but moving money from one purpose to another purpose.

Common Denominator Number One: Purpose

Matt's comment exemplified an individual who works for a cause larger than the task of the day. I was happy to see that he had defined his purpose in altruistic terms. Like a chess player playing three steps ahead, he sees his charter as working for healthy, educated children and safer streets. Matt was able to improve service while cutting costs by fulfilling the human needs of those he served.

Purpose continued to be a popular theme within all the interviews for this book. I heard and felt it loudly when talking to the participants, all of whom were from market-leading organizations. Obviously, at Children's

Hospital and the Mayo and Marshfield Clinics, their purpose, even within IT, is to improve their patients' quality of life. At Harley-Davidson, their role is to help create a lifestyle of freedom. At M&I Bank, they are looking for new approaches to banking like merchant capture, on-line bill payment, and direct deposit. M&I Bank's CEO and Chairman, Dennis Kuester (who started in IT), expressed concern about the single mother who could get stuck in line at 6:00 PM on a Friday when she should be with her children. Purposeful discussions popped up without solicitation in these market leading organizations. In the Wisconsin's case, it is hard to define any government entity as *market leading*. However, they are very well respected among peers for being ahead of the curve.

The cultures of the strongest IT organizations understood clearly the purpose of meeting the human needs of those they served. The most successful IT leaders seemed to think about it constantly. I am not only referring to serving the human needs of the user, but serving the human needs of an organization's consumer. These are two very important but different purposes. Most in IT have one; the best have both.

Level-One Purpose and Level-Two Purpose

As I prepared for my next encounter with Charlie, the IT Director challenged to find his place among his organization's strategic thinkers, I devised a way to classify the notion of purpose for him. For those in IT, there are two types of purpose:

Level-one purpose (L1) serves the human needs of your company's customers.

Level-two purpose (L2) serves the user community within your organization.

Just about every IT organization I have visited in the last few years has a very good handle on their L2 purpose. Most individuals in IT recognize that without serving the users of their organization, their job will not exist. L2 focuses on producing productive, secure, and well-supported users.

When done well, serving at L2 can be very rewarding for all entities. You may find yourself servicing happy users with good morale throughout the ITO. Life is good, right? Sometimes it is too good. Contentment at L2 can hinder one's ambition to understand L1. This is where contentment can become complacency. Remember, L1 and L2 are not roles or positions—they designate levels of understanding of an organization's real purpose.

Almost everyone knows of someone who was happy and enjoying a good life when they were surprised to learn that their company was bankrupt or doing massive cuts because of poor business performance. I am not implying that every one of these tragedies could have been saved by a L1 IT organization. I will suggest, though, that if everyone in IT clearly understood their customers' real needs and was innovating better than the competition to serve them, many could be avoided.

As noted earlier, those who have the most opportunity have investigated and internalized the level-one purpose (L1). Those who get L1 are more likely to exist more in a "want to" versus "have to" environment. Who has the job and who has the career? Is it the developer who has been tasked to modify code in his program or the developer who is modifying code so that infants get their medicine precisely delivered in order to live? I saw specific examples of the latter example in the cultures of Marshfield Clinic and Wheaton Franciscan Healthcare while conducting my interviews.

For the IT individuals and organizations that work hard to perpetuate an understanding of level-one purpose, there are many benefits. Knowing the human-need purpose that the company serves can:

- *Clarify and prioritize issues*—IT planning and prioritization is difficult. Decisions seldom are black and white. Meeting the human needs of your company's customers can clarify the necessary challenges and decisions.

- *Provide the catalyst for real IT innovation*—Those who has been in IT for a while has learned that the value of IT is in direct proportion to its alignment to a company's strategy and purpose. Real IT innovation refers to serving the needs of a company's customers, not just its users. This is important to understand. IT professionals can be happy and innovate ways of serving users, all while the company is going out of business. For an ITO to be great, leadership must happen at all levels regardless of hierarchy. Everyone involved should be making suggestions on how they can create a better client experience, provide better decisional data, serve more customers, and compete among or above market leaders on their industry. Those are examples of decisions that affect a business's value.

- *Mitigate risk*—There is no shortage of case studies about organizations that became slaves to their IT applications. Purpose and a positive customer experience should drive your applications and process, not the other way around. Failure to recognize this creates risk in many ways. These debacles happen less in L1 ITOs.

- *Create good morale*—Writing in *Fortune* magazine, Geoffrey Colvin notes, "One trend in business is that employees, especially young employees, want a sense of purpose in their work. We all want a sense of purpose in our lives, but in the past we didn't demand it from our jobs. Now workers increasingly do. They want to know that what they do at work is good and right in some large sense." Morale issues tend to vanish when everybody focuses on the difference they are making in the lives of others.

- *Secure your company's future*—Remember the second meaning of "while you can" in this book's title. We live in a global market where consumers can research, collaborate, innovate, shop, and sell online. If IT is not helping to drive a company's strategy and competitive advantage, it will become increasingly difficult for that company to be secure in the long term. Get out of IT and into your industry while you can, or your company's long-term success may be jeopardized.

Do We Ever Really Arrive?

Although we never completely arrive, we can take steps to bridge the gap to a better state. Outside of the ITO, there is no shortage of resources dedicated to helping people improve their mind, body, and spirit. My charter is to help IT professionals find success, purpose, and contentment within their livelihood. Ultimately, achieving these will help IT professionals drive organizational and individual success.

Telling people to "get out of IT while you can" is not to imply they shouldn't work in an IT organization or the industry. On the contrary, I perceive that the brightest opportunities for a better future exist in this space. However, to be excellent, individuals need to spend time *while they can* out of the trees to better see the forest. They should allocate time to understand the purpose for their organization, its competitive landscape, how market leaders are aligning IT to their strategies, and how they can improve process- and client-impacting solutions. You will find that the rewards are huge for those who establish such goals. In upcoming chapters there are some simple activities that can make this growth easier.

Chapter Two: Action Items/Points to Ponder

Open up your calendar and schedule one to two hours in the next week to respond to the following L1/L2 questions. It will help if you can get a copy of your company's annual report, strategic plan, and mission statement prior to this time.

L1/L2 questions
Replace the variables in the following statement:

The human-need purpose my company serves is to take x people (current clients) from a y state (current state) to a z state (desired state).

_____

_____

_____

Is this evident in your IT organization's mission statement?_____

If not, review and compare the company's mission statement to that of your IT organization/team. Does the company's customer get lost? Are there suggestions you might make to leadership to amend this?

_____

_____

_____

The absence of a basic business education or decent mentoring can make the journey to L1 seem daunting for some. What can you do within your IT organization to help colleagues get this important perspective?

_____

_____

_____

Point to Ponder:

Do you know a friend or family member who is a customer? Can you ask them about the purpose of their patronage and whether there is something you can start, stop, or think about doing to make serve that purpose better?

Involve as many colleagues as possible in talking the purpose—the purpose of your team, work unit, functional area, region, or even the organization as a whole. Ask, "Why are we in business? Beyond cranking out great products and services and making money, what is our core reason for being?" Leadership is needed at your level, whatever that is.

NOTES

<u>NOTES</u>

The Little I, Big I Scale

Chapter Three

Life is too short to be little.

—Benjamin Disraeli

Chapter Three: Little i or Big I

The next time Charlie and I got together, I explained the types of purposes we serve in IT. Once he could articulate his organization's Level One (L1) purpose, I took him further down the path of growth.

So that he could be the best in his industry, I shared with him what I call my *Little i/Big I Scale.* I tactfully mentioned that his historical tendency has been to exist on the left side of this scale. A "Little i" person is more "in IT" than in their employer's industry. A "Big I" person works in IT, but also sees themselves in the industry of their employer. Without understanding their employer's industry, one's business value and innovation would be low. Certainly, the message could be offensive if I was implying he was one or the other. No one is, I assured him. The truth is that we tend to exist somewhere on this scale. A conscious choice could move us into a better position. I also shared that the scale can be applied to each individual in an IT organization, or to the IT organization as a whole.

As it relates to an ITO, it could be within a company of any size. You could have a one-person company where the president/CIO/janitor is using IT to drive a competitive advantage in their industry (Big I). Conversely, you could have a huge company with a Little i culture that is forfeiting any prospective advantages that come from the right use of IT (Little i). Few people exist at any certain point on this scale; rather, most people fit into a range.

I have been extremely fortunate to watch many people in ITOs break through and mature toward being a Big I employee. The benefits of such growth are numerous. It doesn't need to be difficult. Let's go to the whiteboard and see.

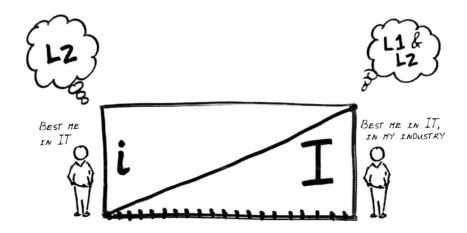

My message is conveyed with sympathy and concern for those whose personal development and IT culture have enabled them to exist indefinitely on the left side of this scale. Many fine individuals may indeed come up on the left side of the scale. This is not an indictment of character. I would not publish this message if I thought that people were hard-wired and should be permanently categorized. The following chapters of this book will show how one can easily move to the right side of this scale.

Historically, ITOs have been built by technical people who were passionate about providing good support. This inherently establishes the IT department's culture. I have respect and appreciation for these people who got us here with passion. I am not writing just about the well-known leaders, but the opinion leaders in the trenches who work tirelessly to solve problems. They were and are still so important. I am sympathetic for those who are now being challenged beyond their comfort zone to see themselves as business leaders. I concur with the cartoon character Pogo, "The certainty of misery is better than the misery of uncertainty." If those same leaders continue to grow, will things fall between the cracks? Will they need to forfeit a solution that they gave birth to?

Get out of IT While You Can will, I hope, create progress for those for whom I am most sympathetic. This book is dedicated to those who want to grow. Just remember, there are thousands of IT people who served an always-on, well-supported user base while their company went bankrupt. We in IT need to help secure our company's' future.

Little i/Big I

The scale is *not* to be applied to an individual's role, but how far they choose to understand the bigger picture and provide progress. Regardless of their position in an IT department, most IT professional seem to be living out a charter. That charter falls within various ranges:

On the left side of the scale is the *Little i*. These individuals (or ITOs) do not see beyond the procurement, implementation, and support of information technology that their company utilizes.

- *Focus: Solely User Satisfaction*
- *Business Innovation: Low*

On the right side is the *Big I*. These individuals (or ITOs) strive to understand their employer's business strategy and industry. They look to drive that purpose and strategy within their career.

- *Focus: Attaining/maintaining market leadership for employer*
- *Business Innovation: High*

Somewhere in the middle is the *Mid I*. These individuals (or ITOs) apply information technology to improve the way critical business functions are being performed. This may include doing all things that a good Little i does well.

- *Focus: Business Unit Satisfaction*
- *Business Innovation: Medium*

More on the Little i

It would be easy to assume by this definition that a Little i exists within purchasing, break-fix, help desk, or networking departments. However, Little i has nothing to do with organizational rank or responsibilities. There are thousands of Little-i types in high-ranking positions. Charlie, my IT director friend, was a Little i. There are many types of Little-i people, but I will discuss the most common forms.

First on the list are those so immersed in technology and the IT organization that they cannot see the business. This could be because their career started and matured in IT without any real business education. This also occurs commonly because everyone in IT is so busy that they don't have time to study the bigger picture. If such an individual is stuck within an ITO culture that doesn't take time to perpetuate understanding of the bigger picture, they may remain a Little i indefinitely. (In fairness, there is a shortage of free time at work for anyone in IT.)

Another common type of Little i *is* interested in the business. They are in the ITO, but not technically savvy at all. Therefore, instead of using their energy to apply IT resources to drive business objectives, they focus primarily on cost reduction. Not everyone in an ITO needs to be technically savvy, but those that aren't should instead look at how market-leading peers are applying technology to drive business objectives. All of us in IT are continually chartered to reduce our organization's cost-per-capacity ratio. However, spending most of one's time commoditizing solutions without showing their colleagues how they are going to succeed strategically is tragic.

There are Little i types that are innovative; however, they spend all of their creative abilities trying to justify/fulfill past decisions instead of getting out of the box to see different approaches. They might look out from where they are (with good intent) to improve current conditions. However, if they fail to start with a desirable endpoint in mind, they may only produce less than desirable results.

As stated previously, a characteristic of a Little i is a low drive for business innovation. Think about existing within any of these defined Little i mindsets. It is understandable how a person might be conditioned to feel that cost containment and risk mitigation as a charter is above business innovation. And rightly so: if business leadership doesn't see you innovating to drive specific business outcomes, they will ask you to focus on cost reduction. Yet, in every interview I conducted with business executives for this book, all said that they would provide "non-budgeted" financial support for real business ideas coming from IT. (There has to be a real ROI, of course.)

Were you dropped on your head?

I am amazed at how many IT professionals, who were once experts in TCO, now refer to PCs as a commodity because they are cheap (meaning they are purchased on price alone). In our industry, only Dell promotes the commodity message; Gartner, Meta, IBM, HP, and most other vendors still see the bigger picture. Computer hardware has become inexpensive, but that often makes it just a smaller portion of the TCO. While sourcing staff high-five because they saved fifty dollars a box on their "commodity," HR might find itself recruiting 2.75 full time equivalents (FTEs) over the course of the next year to deal with new administrative and technical inefficiencies such as:

- Product inconsistency, which leads to more time spent imaging and larger image libraries
- Increased shipping costs
- Dealing with partial shipments
- Reconciling errant product invoices
- Dealing with increased return authorizations
- Higher failure rates
- Lower warranty reimbursements (more "user-fixable" problems)
- Bigger and more complex part closets (which lead to greater downtime)

Hardware is becoming so inexpensive that you could even call it a throw away, but that doesn't make it a commodity. In IT, focusing all of your efforts on doing things cheaper can leave you in a precarious position. Unless your company's strategy is to be the low-cost provider, you should exert more energy into creating a positive client experience and driving strategy than you do cutting costs.

My HR Director, Todd Radke, shared with me an interesting analogy. Folgers tried to get the cost of coffee down to twenty-five cents a cup. Starbucks exploded onto the scene with three-dollar coffee, but with a new experience as well. Anyone who has watched employees arrive late to the office with a latte in hand, when there was a freshly brewed pot of free coffee in the break area, knows which strategy was more successful. Which of these two currently has a more successful brand?

How do you feel when a phone company calls your house at night with an offer of better savings? The feeling is typically that there is negligible difference between carriers because long-distance phone service is a utility. Along the same lines of thinking, workers with a Little-i mindset are often times viewed as the "utility" aspect of IT by the business units. If you are not applying IT to better serve the needs of the company's customer or increase market share, you are increasingly viewed as a utility. People take for granted what it takes to always be on. There is no business value seen in the utility. It's a given, like phone service or electricity. This is unfortunate. IT is a less mature field, at the same time having more complexities and change than these other industries. Whether the perceivers are right or wrong doesn't matter. Perception is reality, and many of these critics exist in high-ranking positions. Being "on" with good support is no reason for applause.

This being the case, the Little i needs to assume the responsibility for the consequences of creating this perception. It is possible for a Little i to exist for an entire career without ever understanding the human needs their company serves. IT workers maintain servers and fulfill service functions in a utilitarian mode until they break down. Long hours or quick action may heroically save the day for the moment … until the next crisis hits. As a company's infrastructure grows, more and more crises will zap increasing time and energy. As a result, *business innovation* will remain low, even though IT service innovation can be high.

More on the Big I

A Big I can exist at any position in the IT organization. If they are at a low organizational level, they will have a hard time staying there. Demand for IT individuals who take a true interest in the business is high everywhere. However, one must choose to be a Big I to ever get there. Big I types choose to allocate time to learn the business purpose and strategy of their employer. Also, they schedule time to learn how market-leading peers are applying technology to improve their company's position. As a result, these individuals are most likely to help innovate.

Innovation doesn't need to be huge; it can come in the form of small improvements to policies and procedures. Regular innovation, no matter how small, is a key characteristic of a Big I. As a result; a Big I gains respect and credibility over time. Big I types can fluently discuss business competencies and what they are doing to achieve a leadership position among their peers. This builds their confidence and creates opportunity for their advancement and compensation.

Organizational culture can dramatically help IT workers achieve a Big-I state of mind. The biggest of the big realize that competitive advantages no longer come in static formats. Real advantage comes from an organization that can fundamentally recreate itself, or at least do so faster than its competition. As we discuss market-leading organizations later on, you will see that participative culture is common within such companies.

One other note: This book has been written primarily for individuals who work within IT organizations that are not specifically in the IT industry. There are many Big Is in the "IT industry"; especially as IT vendors increasingly focus on vertical industries. They attain this status because they are able to share what market leaders are doing within your business and can sometimes help you become a model to emulate among peers.

In the Middle You Have ...

I would like to think that most IT professionals exist somewhere in the middle of the Little i/Big I scale. The prevalence of *Mid I* types increases as IT organizations dedicate application developers and technical support to specific business units. Mid I types at least become cognizant of a business unit's specific charter and can respond accordingly. Application developers dedicated to business units (or customer-facing initiatives) have an easier time succeeding here because they have the requirement of developing with the "end experience" in mind. This requirement gives them the advantage of spending more time with customer-facing colleagues. One can choose to operate at the Mid I level. However, some Mid I individuals never actually chose to be there. They arrived through the fortune of operating in an organizational structure or mentorship program that developed this trait.

The Scale

Although some IT professionals might exist specifically at one of these three stations, this does not imply that you, the reader, are simply one or the other. Almost all individuals exist within a range on this scale, and unlike the graphic below, that range may not start the very left. The circle can be any size as there are versatile people who can exist at all three stations by choosing. I wanted to build the scale to illustrate the heart of this book's message.

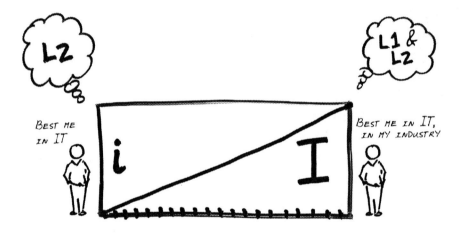

Opportunity and quality of life go up as people grow wider on the scale, or move to the right.

Confidence and compensation come from being respected. Respect comes as you strive to add real business value. It is hard to add business value without understanding the purpose and strategy of your company. Also recognize the integration of L1 and L2 as illustrated above. Understanding the L2 purpose (serving the human needs of a company's customers as well as its user base) tends to help Big Is work in a "want to" versus "have to" mode.

The remainder of the book will show how you can either achieve wider range of L1/L2 function or simply move to the right on this scale. I hope that it will help lead to the above-mentioned benefits.

Where are you on the scale right now?

A CEO's Perspective …

Marshall and Ilsley Corporation (M&I) is a widely respected organization in the banking industry with nearly $40 billion in assets (and growing). Beyond its well-known M&I Banks, M&I Corporation has many subsidiaries that are improving the way banking is done.

I called Dennis Kuester, M&I's chairman, president, and CEO, and asked if I could meet with him to pick his brain for *Get out of IT While You Can*. He knew that I worked within the IT industry and shared that he actually got his start in IT at IBM. I told him that I was trying to assess the many areas of life and business that impacted IT professionals who saw themselves as *in their employers' industry* instead of being *in IT*. His response was quick and strong.

"This really resonates with me," he said. "It is an insidious term—*IT professional!* When people say they are IT professionals, it is as if they can get a job anywhere. They are in banking, healthcare, education, and so forth. It will be hard to add real value until they realize that."

We met again on May 17, 2005 at M&I's Corporate Headquarters in Milwaukee, Wisconsin.

I told Kuester that I felt that he was a bit of an anomaly. Few people start in IT and arrive as a CEO and president of a $40 billion bank.

He responded, "But I never really saw myself as being in IT, always more of a salesman. Let me clarify however, because 'sales' is a term that is often misunderstood. Being in sales is understanding your customers' requirements and how you can best match those requirements. That is what I love to do. Everything starts with customer need. What simplifies their life? What gets them to where they want to go? What is the desired experience? These are the things that must drive our processes, not the applications. When IT is building solutions, they must start with this end in mind, never the other way around."

Dennis went on to say, "There are consummate technologists who desire to be buried in technology. If that is where they want to be, fine. However, the people who are most valuable to us are the ones with IT background who can immerse themselves into the business need. They broaden their experiences and can apply this technology to the business case. These are the ones with real career opportunities. Some can make the transition to other parts of the corporation if they choose to develop the skills that are related to the *business of the business* versus just the *business of IT.*

For example, it is my hope that the IT people assigned to our trust company are trying to understand every facet of that business, even better than what some call trust professionals. They become more valuable, because they understand the value proposition that is being delivered to the customer, not just the user."

Our discussion validated many perceptions that have been shaped through my experience helping our partners in the IT field. Those who see themselves as IT professionals can be perceived as providing less value, and over time, receive less appreciation for their efforts. Those who choose to understand the *real customers* within their business or industry are the most valuable.

The Future Role of IT

I recognize that any distinctive competitive advantages coming from IT solutions are short lived. This is because most competitors have (or will eventually have) access to the same solutions. However, you can't ignore that competitors who are consistently doing a better job of providing good decisional data and unique client experiences are at an advantage. I will argue that even those organizations haven't yet "arrived" with the use of good information.

To be a Big I, you have to not only see the purpose and strategy of the employer, but the role IT has in driving it! This might sound obvious, but it is not.

An article titled CIO Habitat in the June 2005 issue of *CIO Decisions* by Thornton May, states the following.

"In this round of CIO Habitat research, we asked 300 senior IT decision makers to reflect on the next world of IT. Just as we have the red-blue states divide in American politics (with a distribution of approximately 50-50), the technology arena has a similar split, with half believing that IT's role is diminishing (see following Exhibit). These respondents see outsourcing, skills and devices becoming commoditized, with subordination to the financial or compliance function as the next step.

The other half is much more optimistic. These decision makers predicted that resources devoted to IT would actually increase and that IT pros would have an important voice in shaping the future."

But what particularly stood out was how the optimists and pessimists broke down between large- and mid-market enterprises (our sample size was evenly split; 150 large companies, 150 midsized). It would appear in some IT areas, size does matter.

We noted that of all the "IT will dominate in the future" respondents came from A-list, high-performing companies. No real surprise here. What was surprising was that only 35% of these folks from large enterprises fell on the optimistic side, while 65% at smaller (mid-market) companies were optimistic."

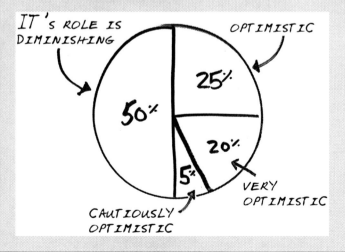

To be a Big I, you must see a future role in IT. One interesting observation I had when reviewing this research, was that mid-market organizations tend to be more optimistic about the role IT will play in their success. If you subscribe to my theory, you will appreciate Rupert Murdoch's quote: **"Big will not beat small anymore. It will be the fast beating the slow."**

> *To be a Big I, you have to see the purpose and strategy of the employer, and the role IT has in driving it!*

Back to Charlie …

I shared my theories and observations with Charlie, the IT director from the beginning of this book. I let him know that management wanted for him what he wanted for himself. This, of course, was for Charlie to be seen as a major contributor to the success of the company. They had respect for him, but his evolution stagnated. From management's perspective, real value had little to do with performing the "utility" aspects of IT (uptime, security, technology refresh, and support). Utilities are supposed to always be on, and are viewed increasingly as a commodity. For Charlie, being viewed as a commodity was no way to find job satisfaction. He now understood that a real contributor could even be an entry-level IT person who takes up the businesses interest, and offers up suggestions on how their competitive position can be improved.

Charlie saw how opportunity and quality of life could go up as he grew wider on the scale, or moved to the right. It wasn't clear how the transformation would take place, but he was willing to commit to it. Our next encounter would focus on moving in the right direction.

Chapter Three: Action Items/Points to Ponder

<u>You</u>

1) Circle your range on the scale below. Where do you feel you are so far?

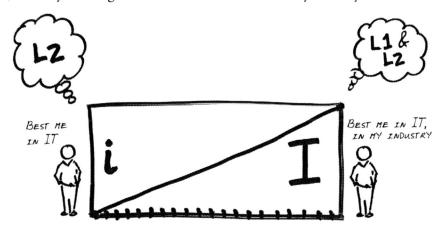

2) Where are you on the Little i/Big I Scale? What is preventing you from moving to the right on the scale? Create a list of three to five things that would help you widen your range on this scale.

_____

_____

_____

_____

_____

<u>Your Company's IT Organizational Culture</u>

3) Circle your company's range on the scale below. Is your company driving a competitive advantage?

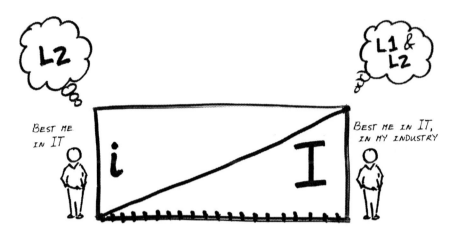

4) Does the majority of your IT organization see the purpose and strategy of your company? Circle where you feel the majority of the ITO exists. Create a list of three to five ideas or accomplishments that would help your organization widen your range on this scale.

_____

_____

_____

_____

_____

NOTES

NOTES

Moving in the Right Direction

Chapter Four

People often say that this or that person has not found himself. But the self is not something that one finds. It is something one creates.

—Thomas Szasz

Chapter Four: Moving in the Right Direction

For the purposes of an imaginary exercise, randomly choose someone in your IT organization and picture them in your mind. This could be you or anyone at any level within the ITO. You could also choose someone from HR, finance, or administration, as this book could be applied to getting out of HR, finance or administration as well.

Do you have someone in mind?

Now imagine your CEO grabbing that person in the hallway at work and saying, "I really need your help! A group of prospective customers is here for a tour of our organization, and we would really like to get their business. I was supposed to give the tour, but an emergency came up, and I have to leave. Would you please give them the tour and overview of our organization?

"Don't stress," she says assuringly. "They will probably just ask you some basic questions. You know, questions like

- Who does and doesn't your company serve?
- Compared to your competition, what are your company's core competencies?
- Why do you think the client experience here is better than the competition?
- How does your industry measure excellence, and how do you rate?
- What will be the main differences in five years from now in your organization?
- Oh, you are in IT? What are you doing to drive your company's strategy and client experience?
- How is your company innovating or investing in the future to ensure long-term viability?

"You know, that kind of stuff. Thank you, thank you, thank you," the CEO continues as she heads down the hall. You hear in the distance a final remark, "Thank God everyone is in sales. It will be great for us to get this business."

No pressure, right?

As you take your candidate through this exercise, how did the tour aspect go? Consider the following questions:

- Did he or she clearly know the facilities and charters of each department?
- How strong and succinct was the answer content for the questions asked by the prospects?
- How well did they differentiate your offering in comparison to the competitions (without bad-mouthing the competition)?
- Prospects don't buy your products and services; they buy your belief in your products and services. Did you candidate have enough understanding, belief, and enthusiasm to close the deal?

What a great litmus test! This helps identify where individuals are on the Little i/Big I scale. The CEO's comment, "Everyone is in sales," should be true to a great extent. To be in sales, you have to believe in your market offering in comparison to the competition. I know many professionals do not see this as part of their job, just as many see their occupation as a job instead of a career. It is interesting how many highly competitive people do not see their role as helping their employer compete.

Moving to the right side of the Little i/Big I scale is an effort that could pay handsome dividends, not just create more homework. Those who strive to understand the rationale behind their organizations strategy, purpose, and competitive stance enjoy their work more while driving more value. It feels like less to deliver more.

> *We cannot live better than in seeking to become better.*
>
> —*Socrates*

Quad/graphics

IT individuals can drive and sell their organization. I asked for a tour of Quad/graphics from one of my contacts in their IT department. Quad/graphics is the third-largest printing company in the United States, having about $2 billion in revenues.

I was interested in a tour not because of my background in IT, but as a CEO who wanted to understand what made Quad/graphics so successful. I was measuring its success by both its continual recognition as one of the best places to work and its consistent growth.

My tour guide was Steve Jaeger, the VP of Information Services and Infrastructure. As we walked around one of their locations, I got an overview of all that transpires, seeing raw materials transform into products just as they arrive at the readers' doors. As I looked at their finished products, it seemed that just about every magazine on earth must be printed by them.

My tour guide enthusiastically showed me how "Quad" was innovating to improve printing and logistics within its industry. He clearly understood the role of all areas of the organization. He shared how all areas toured were yielding distinctive competitive advantages.

I then asked him, "How is IT is innovating to yield competitive advantages?"

Without skipping a beat, he said, "It's all about data! IT is very strategic here; in fact, we even generate revenues: QuadData Solutions has revenues of about $12 million. We have developed ink-jetting solutions so our customers can individualize literature for their clients. We have developed integrated publishing solutions which help our client's 'publishing teams' collaborate better. We help drive production planning, advertising, and production management, and give our clients significantly better decisional data." Steve then shared that their Quad/Tech division developed solutions that their competitors were buying from them. What a validation of competitive advantage it is when competitors or peers buy products you have developed internally.

I love going on organizational tours, and this was one of my favorites. I saw a culture that educates and innovates all over the company. Over time I have met several people within Quad's ITO. It came to mind that although I was fortunate to have Steve as my guide, many other professionals within their IT organization could have given a great tour as well. Everyone I met was excited about how they are improving printing and service of their clients.

Moving in the Right Direction Doesn't Take Much

In my last conversation with my friend, Charlie, I shared with him the "best you in your employer's industry" concept. I challenged him to see the human-need purpose his employer served. I let him know that changing one's mindset from a being a Little i to a Big I isn't that hard, but it takes a little commitment and time.

Charlie tried to stump me. "If I get out of IT and into my industry, who is going to do my job and support my infrastructure? My users?" I was glad he asked this important question. He assumed that I was telling him to get out of his role. I was not. Being a little more industry-focused can be life-altering, but doesn't need to be world-shattering. Recognize that in the analogy at the beginning of Chapter Two, the ditch digger and the hospital builder are doing the same job. I replied to Charlie, "You will do your job for now."

Moving to the right requires as little as twenty to thirty minutes a week. Schedule it in whatever calendar system you use. In *Get out of IT While You Can*, the "while you can" means it is necessary to have regularly scheduled time to get into your employer's purpose, strategy, and industry.

There are some fundamental assignments that you should impose on yourself. Don't wait for your boss to tell you—remember, leadership happens at all levels. To ensure that you are at least in Middle I territory, tackle *the Mid-I list*:

- Read your annual report. (Week One)
- Study your strategic plan. (Week Two)
- Make your own list of things that need to evolve in IT to drive the strategy. (Week Three)
- Review your Web site and marketing collateral. (Week Three)
- Discuss findings and/or suggestions for improvement to colleagues.

Then move on to competitive landscape, market leaders and best practices.

- Look at your primary competitors' Web site, annual reports, and strategic implications. How they are using IT to drive better client experience or increased market share? Remember, if you don't think it is your responsibility to help compete, you won't.

- Look at industry-leading peers' Web sites, annual reports, and strategic implications. Don't be shy about getting inspired by a market leader. Pablo Picasso once said; Invent as a last resort: "Good artists borrow, great artists steal."

- How are these organizations using IT to drive better client experience or increased market share?

- Ask your vendors, "What should we start, stop, or think about doing to be great in our industry?" Most vendors are "verticalizing" by industry segment, and if they have both a clue and a backbone, they will have some suggestions for improving your priorities.

- Google "IT best practices" in areas that need improvement. It is humorous how many great ideas are yours for the asking.

- Consider joining an industry IT affiliation organization.

- Job shadow customer-facing staff. This should happen periodically. Good people with good intent can defend the way they do something. And once they see and hear customers, they become open and innovative. At Mayo Clinic, IT staff job shadows 911 operators, receiving and admitting, and even surgeries. Then they are chartered with innovating, no matter how small, to improve their delivery.

- Ask a customer about his or her client experience. What should you start, stop, or think about doing to serve their purpose better? (This can be done continually over time.)

- Examine which IT services are most important to driving your company's business. (This can also be done continually.)

- Finally, share, share, and share your evolving perceptions with colleagues. Leadership happens at every level. No matter what your role, you should lead by example.

We are talking about *a choice*. Those professionals who have the best quality of life, add the most value, and grow the most, choose these meaningful charters. They choose to set specific, time-bound goals to accomplish relevant objectives. Believe me, the Mid-I checklist is relevant. Getting to your desired state is your choice.

You Have a Responsibility

If you are in charge of employee reviews, then assign these exercises. You have a wonderful responsibility to help your employees grow personally and professionally. Assign these exercises, then organize a small group discussion to discuss how your department can drive more business value or competitive advantage.

Conversely, if you are going into your annual review with your boss, establish specific goals ahead of time. Go in prepared to discuss purpose, strategy, the competitive landscape, and tasks you should start, stop, or think about doing. I don't just want you to understand your company and how you can help drive strategy, but how you can help your company compete in its peer group. This is where you can add great value. We will discuss this in the next chapter, "Play to Win."

The Second Renaissance

Terrorism and natural disasters notwithstanding, now is the best time to be alive. There is no shortage of people who romanticize about life during the Renaissance. Yet today we exist in a second renaissance where possibilities for innovation and advantage are endless. Gutenberg's press catalyzed the original renaissance. Information and ideas could be shared faster than ever before. Entrepreneurs of that era were able to spark economic prosperity like never before—not just writers, but anyone interested in advancing themselves. People could learn from broader range of resources as well as each other's mistakes.

We are now in the second renaissance. Anyone with initiative can advance themselves easier than ever before. The overbuilding of infrastructure (which sank companies like Enron and MCI) has given as many as four billion people access to the Internet. Libraries and industrial research are accessible to anyone with a Web browser. For example, when I searched Google for "IT Help Desk Best Practices," I received 8,300,000 articles in .21 seconds.

This technology enables us to research, learn from others' mistakes, collaborate, and possibly spark original ideas. Unlimited business opportunities are available for those with the enterprise to do so.

I think another variable that makes this renaissance more beautiful is that there is less prejudice in it. I would like to think that this ugly issue doesn't exist, but that would be naïve. I do believe though that there is more equality now than there was in the last renaissance. As a result, good and righteous ideas from anywhere have greater possibility of finding a home. This is an important improvement.

I am convinced that three hundred years from now, people will be discussing the victors of the second renaissance. There will be countless stories of entrepreneurs who leveraged these resources to their maximum benefit. This opportunity is yours. By opportunity, I don't necessarily mean that you have to search online for a new career or company. You can use this resource to find ways to add more value to your present job. The benefits will come.

One can certainly argue that there is too much information out there to navigate. I would side with that argument; however, that is no justification for the discontent to become complacent. The same discontented individuals who are criticizing the work ethic of youth today have a laptop that can get them to a better livelihood if they exhibit a little work ethic right now.

As I previously acknowledged, a career path for today's IT professional can be void of business training. Diligently completing these exercises can offer you an education beyond that of many of today's business graduates. You will soon be in a position to help drive strategy and competitive stance.

Chapter Four: Action Items/Points to Ponder

1) Moving in the right direction requires committing to concrete goals. As you review the suggestions of the Mid-I list, also answer the questions below. First come questions about your organization. Next are questions about its competitive landscape. Remember to assign yourself these questions when you are preparing for a review. Are you ready to give the company tour to key prospects?

Who is our target customer base?

_____

What need are we trying to fulfill?

_____

Independent of price, what gives us a loyal customer base?

_____

What are our two to three distinctive competencies or competitive advantages?

_____

What about our organization would we like to be industry leading in thirty-six months

_____

How big do we want to be in thirty-six months? (Consider geographic trading area, revenues, employees, etc.)

_____

What does my company need or want to make this happen?

_____

What are our biggest obstacles to success?

_____

Does the IT organization understand how they are contributing to our companies/clients strategic vision?

_____

What is our thirty-second elevator pitch (commercial) to give to a prospective client?

_____

Competitive Landscape/Industry Questions

2) Who is our primary competition?

How are they applying IT to create a great customer experience?

How are they applying IT to control costs or mitigate risks?

What can be learned by comparing our organization to theirs (both the ITO and the entire organization)?

3) Who is the market-leader in our industry?

What are their specific competencies?

What are their competitive advantages?

Independent of price, how are they trying to create a loyal customer base?

What are their weaknesses?

Assume the IT organization of a "market leader" has a clear vision, what do you suppose theirs is?

How are they applying IT to create great customer experience?

How are they applying IT to control cost or mitigate risks?

What can be learned by comparing your organization to theirs (entire and ITO specific)?

_____

_____

How can you share lessons learned with colleagues?

_____

_____

Point to Ponder:

What does the graphic at the beginning of this chapter imply? It is not a picture of a Leading IT organization with a Little i on the right. The picture represents a Big I beside his Board of Directors. This person is *moving in the right direction*. He has completed the Mid-I list.

One could argue that he looks like he is doing Little-i stuff, but he is becoming a Big I. He just got done congratulating the Board on their recent industry accolade. He is growing into a new role. At his neighborhood BBQ party, a new neighbor asked him what he does for a living. He responded, *"I am in healthcare."* When the neighbor inquired further, he shared that he worked at the clinic in their IT department.

To move in the right direction and get into your industry, consider joining an Industry IT Affiliation. Go to http://www.getoutofit.net for a list of IT associations by industry.

NOTES

NOTES

Play to Win vs. Play Not to Lose

Chapter Five

Innovation distinguishes between a leader and a follower
—Steve Jobs

It's easy to have faith in yourself and have discipline when you're a winner, when you're Number One. What you've got to have is faith and discipline when you're not yet a winner.

—Vince Lombardi

Chapter Five: Play to Win vs. Play Not to Lose

Playing to win is about achieving success through innovation. It starts with taking your understanding of your organization's purpose, strategy, and market position and doing something with it. Remember that a key characteristic of the Big I is business innovation. The place to start is in your mindset.

Mindsets

I was conversing recently with a colleague and good friend, Chris Liburdi. I asked about his weekend, and he told me that he went to Las Vegas with his wife's company. I asked him if he gambled, and if so, did he win or lose. He responded, "I didn't lose, but I was thinking on the plane back, that I wasn't playing to win; I was playing not to lose."

I congratulated Chris for not losing in Vegas. I walked away thinking that there wasn't a big difference between "playing to win" and "playing not to lose". Then I began to see all around me the two mindsets in action and their related outcomes. In my community, family, church, and work, it appeared that most people were playing not to lose. In IT organizations, I could see individuals who *play to win* in all other aspects of their life, yet *play not to lose* at work. It became clear that fear of failure is the most common catalyst for choosing the *play not to lose* mindset.

As it is with Little i/Big I, no one is hardwired to be a winner or loss-avoider. Although everyone has their tendencies, they can still choose their path. Here is an excellent example of how one person can choose to play either to win or not to lose. It is a choice!

You see it in sports every week

You might think I have issues, but I admit that I watch golf tournaments on TV from time to time. It is an occasional activity that I enjoy with my father-in-law. He and I were watching the Fed Ex St. Jude Classic in late May of 2005. In this particular tournament, former British Open Champion Justin Leonard was crushing the field with all aspects of his game. He played to win aggressively for the first three days and found himself with an eight-stroke lead going into the final day. No one has ever lost a tournament going into the final day with an eight-stroke lead. He was in great shape.

On the match's last day, it seemed to me that Justin took the course as a completely different player. Because of his sizable lead, perhaps he went into "just play safe" mode. He then proceeded to hit only five of eighteen greens in regulation. His mindset seemed to change. Justin had been playing some of the best golf of his career for the last three days. Now it seemed he was abandoning that style of play for a safer style that quickly began to fail him. He was not having fun at all as he found himself playing worse than par while his lead quickly dwindled. He had to know that he was close to entering the record books for blowing the biggest lead ever on the PGA tour.

As a fan of Justin Leonard, I am happy to say that he made a three-foot putt to avoid going into a sudden death play-off with David Toms. He then collapsed on the green, having learned how exhausting playing "not to lose" can be. He thought he would play comfortably, and the result was anything but comfortable

I appreciated that Chris could put his "winning vs. loss avoidance" theory into words. It brings to light the idea that you can train your inner dialogue to catch you when you are feeling excessively fearful. In IT organizations, we have to both play not to lose and play to win to be successful. Both mindsets are very essential attributes of a good IT organization. There must be a balance. However, only one drives true business value.

In <u>IT:</u>—*Play not to lose* <u>characteristics don't expand much beyond:</u>
- Cost reduction
- Cost avoidance
- Risk mitigation

IT *Play to win* <u>characteristics you add to the above characteristics:</u>
- Driving the business
- Driving its strategy

IT professionals need to adopt both approaches to be successful. Now and forever, we in IT will be chartered with looking for ways of providing more capacity for less cost. However, if most of your creative resources are applied to cost and risk avoidance, you will not deliver the greatest value to your company. This also demonstrates the "not to lose" tendency of individuals and ITOs that spend most of an initiative's time upfront identifying every conceivable risk (or cost to be avoided) instead of driving business value (client experience, competitive position, market share, etc.). What a wasted opportunity!

All initiatives should first establish how the business can successfully measure its impact in the marketplace. Failure to do so will have the finance department demanding a "play not to lose" mindset from the outset (which, unfortunately, becomes self-perpetuating).

Winners want to help build a company that their clients don't want to live without. They take their understanding of purpose, strategy, and the competitive landscape and continually look for ways (no matter how small) to improve their company's position. The goal is to be good in your industry, not just good compared to how you used to be. It is about creating customer loyalty, not just customer satisfaction. It is about knowing what you don't want to be. Above all, playing to win is about innovation and fostering the culture that allows it. I shared this theory in one of my keynote speeches; shortly thereafter, someone sent me the following article by Ann Vertel:

Ask yourself if you are playing to win or playing to *not lose*.

Aren't they the same thing? No way. Most people play not to lose, in order to avoid fear or pain. "I'll play, as long as I don't get hurt." They will go all the way out to the edge of their comfort zone ... and stop. When you play to not lose, you let fear stop you dead in your tracks. Fear of rejection, failure, successes, disapproval, not measuring up, being uncomfortable, making a mistake, getting hurt, or looking foolish. Anytime you hear yourself say, "I can't," what you really mean is, "I'm afraid."

Wildly successful high-earners play to win.

- They love winning far more than they hate losing.
- They focus on winning.
- They do not focus on "not losing."

And here's a secret lots of people don't know:

Wildly successful people are scared all the time. Why? Because they are always operating outside of their comfort zones. They are always taking risks. Fear never goes away; they just get used to feeling it.

Everything you are going after is outside your comfort zone. Turn toward the fear and play to win.
—Ann Vertel, MA, CPBA Marketing Consultant and
Business Development Coach

The great thing about the message Ms. Vertel and I share is that people do not inherently embody one position or the other, but in fact it is a choice or a tendency. You can decide when you want to put which hat on! We are not hardwired.

Courage is fear that has said its prayers.
—*Karl Barth, Swiss Theologian*

A great take-away is that winners have the same fears, but they love winning more than they hate losing. They love the respect that comes from innovating or driving company success. This can drive behavior more than fear of failure for winners. They come to recognize that worrying is the most useless emotion on earth. Can you train your inner dialogue to face the fear? It is complacency not to try!

One factor that perpetuates the "play not to lose" existence is self-doubt in one's business acumen. Some IT professionals can fluently answer the assigned questions from the end of Chapter Four, and yet set aside that knowledge for fear of looking stupid. How tragic is that? If you have chosen to understand your company's charter and market position, you now have the responsibility and privilege of doing something great. It is called innovation. And now we are really moving in the right direction.

Of the numerous definitions of *innovation* found online, this one jumped out at me:

> *Innovation:* The conversion of knowledge and ideas into a benefit, *which may be for commercial use or for the public good; the benefit may be new or improved products, processes, or services. Innovation and technological change are without doubt the main drivers of economical growth.*
>
> —Creative Commons

What does "Innovation is a common characteristic on the right side" mean? As your awareness of your opportunities expanded with the lessons from the prior chapter, you committed to the goal of more clearly understanding your organization and how it hopes to compete in the future. Just by clarifying your perceptions, you are moving in the right direction. Are you going to take your knowledge and ideas and turn them into a benefit?

Now let your professional career be defined by your periodic suggestions on how to improve your organization.

Big-I Innovation Questions

What can you or your ITO do to help:
- Drive customer experience?
- Drive customer loyalty?

- Drive strategy or remove obstacles to it?
- Drive capture of additional market share?
- Provide better decisional data to sales and management?
- Foster a culture of innovation?
- Measure success?

As you've incorporated the Mid-I exercises into your professional schedule, do so with the Big-I innovation exercises. If you are mentoring individuals, help them set specific time-based goals. If you are your own mentor, be prepared to offer some suggestions to drive these objectives. How are *you* building a company that customers would not want to be without? Innovation and agility: these are worthy goals! Your job is to help perpetuate this mindset. The majority of innovation in the average IT organization is attempts to do more with less instead of helping the company compete. If you could pick one of these to achieve, what would it be? Can you do both? All IT professionals should be asking themselves and their coworkers these questions.

Let innovation, no matter how small, be one of your defining characteristics.

Innovation: Fostering the environment

It was one of the shortest interviews I conducted for this book. Still, it powerfully illustrated the characteristics of a market-leading organization.

I went to the Mayo Clinic in Rochester, Minnesota, to meet Mark Henderson, the section head of Technology Support Services. The Mayo Clinic is recognized as the world leader in healthcare and healthcare research. I had known Mark for many years and was always impressed by the maturity of his IT organization. By this, I mean not the quality of its support model, toolsets, and policies and procedures, but also the level of purpose and humility exhibited by Mark and his team. To me, they had always seemed extremely innovative as well. Ideas start in Mayo's IT department that their competitors ultimately buy from them. I wanted to know more about Mayo, its culture, and how this affected the IT support organization. What led to and keeps them being ahead of the curve?

There was another reason I was interested in meeting with the infrastructure and support leadership. In all of my travels, I have found that these are the teams the have the most challenge in moving from the little i (in IT) to big I (in industry) mindset.

Outside of our meeting room was a very quiet hall, with nurses and doctors down in the distance going about their tasks. The door was very simple, and looked just like all of those leading into the other hospital rooms. As Mark opened the door for me to enter, I found myself entering what could have been a movie set for *Willy Wonka & the Chocolate Factory*. It was like an oasis for the land of creativity. Mark said, "This is an innovation room." The table looked like a puzzle, the fun lighting above was set amongst clouds, and all of the tools necessary to create a new world order were on hand. They did not spare expenses when building this war room. Obviously here, the war was against status quo, complacency, and mediocrity.

One of the first things I noticed was an article on the wall from the *Wall Street Journal*. On first glance, I read that the Mayo Clinic's culture of innovation led to their market leadership for saving lives. I wanted to get a copy for this project, so I looked at the date of the article—it was from the year 2075. It was an article from the future, looking back at today, painting a picture for everyone currently at Mayo to see the outcome of their choice to innovate today. That is leadership!

With What Budget?!

"Yeah, right, buddy!" "Let's get out of the box and innovate ... with what budget?" "I can't even get funding for my infrastructure project!" These are occasional responses you could expect to hear from even the best leaders in IT organizations. Somehow, they have been conditioned to think that their company will not support creative thinking. I would argue that this is a major misperception in IT today. Business leaders eagerly wait for ideas that drive business value. Nonbudgeted ideas really drive strategy in a realistic fashion; you might be surprised how much support there is in your organization.

While researching this book, I met with senior executives at Children's Hospital, CUNA Mutual, Harley-Davidson, M&I Bank, Marshfield Clinic, Mayo Clinic, Quad/graphics, and the State of Wisconsin. I asked them if they could get "non-budgeted financial support" for ideas that drove business strategy, customer loyalty, or the capture of market share capture. The answers were unanimous: absolutely! In fact, during my interview with Mark Henderson at the Mayo Clinic, he had to step out of our meeting to obtain $10 million to fund an integration project that was not in the annual budget.

Even in budget-burdened industries like utilities, you can get support, although a hard-dollar payback is required.

My Trip to CUNA Mutual Group

I went to CUNA Mutual Group to talk with Rick Roy, the Chief Information & Technical Officer. The CUNA Mutual Group is the leading provider of financial services to credit unions and their members worldwide, with roughly $2.5 billion in revenues and 6,000 employees (700 within IT). Rick shared both excitement and frustration about business innovation in IT. He was excited about those individuals who contributing to his company's continual growth and evolution. But he was frustrated that many still don't see (or believe) that it's their responsibility to innovate. He showed me the graphic below, which he created to explain how CUNA's IT investments are shifting from infrastructure to building new capabilities in business systems.

"The first challenge for those 'in infrastructure' is that they are continually chartered to provide more for less," Rick said. "The second challenge is that they have to fight conditioning that says there is not funding to do other things … things that provide business value. The funding exists, but we have to shift our investments to things that drive value and agility"

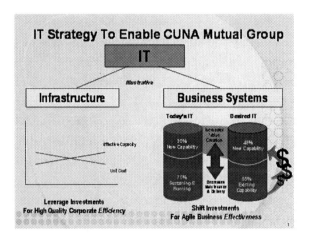

I think Rick's graphic clearly illustrates what I consistently see in ITOs. Companies are shifting their investments from infrastructure to initiatives that visibly drive value. If you want to get out of the "more for less" existence, start answering the "play to win" questions in this book. Of course, I am not telling you get out of infrastructure, but instead to innovate from wherever you are, and opportunity will follow. Opportunity also follows those who help perpetuate the culture of agility from wherever they are.

Playing to Win

This notion is the culmination of all our lessons so far. After moving in the right direction and internalizing your company's strategy, face the fear of failure and choose to innovate. You need to look for ways, no matter how small, to help drive strategy and client experience. You need to trust that there might be more financial support for good ideas than you might believe in your organization.

You need to help build a company that you target customers don't want to be without. That's customer loyalty! That is the underlying variable of organizations that can sustain success.

The difference between customer satisfaction and customer loyalty

Have you ever been satisfied with both a car you purchased and the store where you bought it? Does that mean that you will commit to giving them all of your future business? Does that mean that you strongly recommend them to your friends? Most consumers can be satisfied, but not necessarily loyal. You probably have a better example from your own experiences about a time you were satisfied, but not necessarily inspired to loyalty. I would like you to take a minute to think about it.

First, recognize that it is difficult for your company to have loyal customers if you and your fellow employees are not driving this quality. Customer loyalty can't be bought; it must be earned. When I ask you to "build loyalty," I am asking you to establish accountability for your clients' experiences. Success, as defined by sustainable growth and profitability, is most likely to occur when your customers recommend your products and company to friends and family.

Suggest to your IT leadership that you should assemble some small groups to discuss the ultimate customer experience and how you can drive it. By doing so, you will also develop a loyal, and not just satisfied, boss.

Remember my friend Chris Liburdi from the beginning of the chapter? Before I move on, I have to share an update on his most recent trip to Las Vegas. In passing, I learned that he went again to Las Vegas, so of course I inquired about his fortune. He responded, "I won! I did very well, but I played to win this time." Congratulations, Chris, but stop while you're ahead. Vegas is different from the real world☺!

Chapter Five: Action Items/Points to Ponder

1) What obstacles or fears must be overcome to effectively suggest ways that your ITO can help:

- Drive customer experience?

_____

_____

- Drive customer loyalty?

_____

_____

- Drive strategy or remove obstacles to it?

_____

_____

- Drive capture of additional market share?

_____

_____

- Foster a culture of innovation?

_____

_____

2) If there are obstacles, list them. Are they real or perceived? Can you face them on your own? Can a colleague help eliminate these obstacles?

3) Here are some *Play to Win* questions that real contributors in IT tend to ask themselves. Establish a realistic time-bound goal to go through the list. Perhaps tackle one to three questions weekly.

As with the Mid-I questions: If you are mentoring others, assign these questions to foster the culture of innovation. If you are going into a review, be prepared to answer some of them. Also, consider having brainstorming session with colleagues to discuss these questions and good prospective responses.

Play-to-Win Questions

You should ask yourself continually …

1) What do our customers value most?

2) How can I contribute to that value proposition?

3) How can I help improve the customer experience?

4) What percentage of our clients refers friends to us?

5) How can I help drive customer loyalty?

6) Can IT be used to improve the rate at which we capture market share?

7) Of all of the IT solutions we provide, what three are most important to driving the business of the company?

8) How must we evolve IT to drive our strategic plan? Which of these are we not doing well currently?

9) If we were selling our IT solutions externally, what would our competitors buy from us? Are these the solutions that drive the business?

10) Where should we hone our focus in order to drive competitive advantage?

11) What is the best way of clearly helping our IT organization understand their role in driving the business?

12) What stands in our way of providing solutions to these types of questions?

13) How can I help perpetuate a culture of innovation and agility?

14) Through this exercise, what was the hardest thing to find out about my company's strategy? Should I suggest how this can be made more accessible?

15) How can I bridge a stronger alignment with the business side of my employer?

16) Independent of financial support, what are my obstacles to innovation?

17) Is there something I can do to address these obstacles?

18) If my IT organization was starting all over today, what wouldn't I build and maintain that I had to (or did) in the past?

19) What are the best ways to suggest bridging gaps between current and desired states?

20) How am *I* building a company that customers would not want to be without?

Point to Ponder Consider a project that you were actively involved in. Where did you spend most of your time and emotional energy? Was it up front, identifying every possible risk of moving forward? Are you spending more on the backside to measure and market how it is impacting your business? Planning is essential, but if much more than a third of your time is here, you might be playing not to lose. This ratio isn't always the case, but it is a good rule of thumb. Avoid the falling into an existence where your energy is spent identifying risks of moving forward. You can be missing both opportunity and a better quality of life.

NOTES

NOTES

Leading ITOs

Chapter Six

Leading ITOs are money!
They make money, save money, and create competitive
advantage and agility for their entire organization.
                                        —Craig Schiefelbein

Chapter Six: Leading ITOs

Up until now, *Get Out of IT While You Can* has focused primarily on the role of the individual in the IT organization (ITO). Those who can evolve their understanding of their employer's purpose, industry, strategy, and position in its competitive landscape stand much to gain. These odds go up dramatically if the individual "plays to win" and innovates on behalf of their employer's customer and strategy. All lessons to this point have been designed to move you individually to a better state of purpose and innovation. The remainder of this book is about IT organizations as a whole.

This chapter responds to the second of two questions continually posed to me. The first question is, What does it take to be a successful individual in IT? Hopefully, I have sparked some food for thought in the previous chapters.

The second question is, Of all of the great IT organizations you work with, *what do the best IT organizations look like?* And it's a great question. How do we compare? What should we start, stop, or think about doing within our IT department. Of course the term *IT department* gets interchanged with IS, infrastructure team, ITO, and so forth, depending on the culture of the company.

As in the first portion of this book, I assembled ideas from a number of peers and colleagues to identify qualities that identify top thinkers and their companies. We did recognize that no IT organization has arrived, though a few really stand out though for specific reasons.

I also quickly realized that describing a leading ITO shouldn't be done in a chapter, but an entire book. The next edition of this book, or next book from me, will probably expound greatly upon what I am about to summarize. Currently, I hope to produce a message that helps people immediately instead a creating the perfect message much, much later.

In this chapter, I am opting *not* to map out a hierarchy chart, as most companies have an applications team and infrastructure team reporting upward to the CIO). Nor am I not mapping out a six-step recipe to greatness. I am simply sharing the criteria that surfaced through discussions with CIOs and notable industry veterans when asked, "What makes an IT organization great?" Together we identified components that we felt were strong indicators of success. We couldn't identify any one ITO that completely met all our criteria, but some companies met many or most of these benchmarks quite well. By today's standards, these organizations are the best in our eyes.

We will discuss each of these criteria in length after the summary list. They are, in no particular order:

- Value focus and sourcing strategy
- Revenue generation
- Solid asset management methodology
- Marketing of successes
- Financial and performance measurement.
- Leadership and culture

Value Focus and Sourcing Strategy

IT organizations that add the most value to their respective companies focus on just that: value. They have a commonly understood vision for their IT organization that is understood by its members. Within these teams of individuals, the majority can articulate the difference between strategic and tactical measures. This is because their internal resources are focused on goals that help their employer excel within their industry. Consider these questions:

- Is the difference between strategic and tactical activities and measures commonly understood within your IT department?
- Is it understood what services IT provides that drive the most value?
- Is there a career path that helps individuals move from the tactical to strategic?

I was having a discussion with Jerry Roberts, the CIO for Dean Healthcare (headquartered in Madison, Wisconsin). He reminisced about an era where he and his team "had eyes bigger than their stomachs," to use his grandmother's adage:

"We were determined to do all things great. Certainly we had a great team, great intent, and a strong work ethic, but we also had an ambitious reach. 'Focus' is a subjective term and is relative to differing perceptions.

Initially, we believed we could be great focusing on ten things. After realizing that execution was sub-optimal, we launched an internal campaign called FOCUS. The FOCUS campaign helped colleagues understand the difference between strategic value and tactical tasks. The outcome was a choice to focus on the five things that yielded the most discernable business value to Dean Healthcare. We would collaborate with partners on the remainder. Today, FOCUS is imbedded into our departmental culture. As for collaboration and sourcing, that's been great for us as well, because we have access to critical skill sets while still driving outcomes."

Dean Healthcare is a well-known and respected provider in healthcare because of this type of leadership. They chose to pick both their battles and their allies, and are victorious as a result.

Value focus without a good sourcing strategy will lead to mediocrity. You need to have both, as well as the ability to govern multi-sourced work forces. Can you succinctly articulate your sourcing strategy to your management and colleagues?

The successful leader in IT of yesterday took pride in doing everything themselves. Today, the successful leader takes pride that they have found a way to focus on core business initiatives. They have examined the business strategy and understand what activities in IT will provide the most business value. They have developed a structure and methodology for managing multiple workforces. Beyond measuring their execution, these leaders are receiving improved measurements from their partners, detailing how sourcing has improved time to implementation, service level agreements (SLAs), access to tools and skills, and so forth.

Outsourcing has become a negative term, and it strikes fear in the heart of American workers. However, if you get past the emotion you will have a hard time finding anyone claiming that they can meet all of their IT needs internally. Thriving in IT is increasingly dependent on picking both your battles and your allies.

Sourcing is a competency that needs to be developed and celebrated where possible. Failure to do so may remove it as *your* option to decide. Currently, more and more business units are taking over the sourcing decisions once owned by IT. More than ever, sourcing departments are making product procurement decisions, and service sourcing decisions are being made by business units or non-IT leadership. As this happens, two risks face those unwilling to understand sourcing as a competency.

IT staff that spend their time defending past decisions may find that they are in fact preventing themselves from gaining strategic opportunities. Support staff that refuses to make the jump may find themselves stuck because their strategic initiatives will be owned by other departments. Other times, they can cling to tactical procedures to discover, right or wrong, that their business instead thinks these are commodity solutions that can be better accomplished externally.

Mediocrity is abundant in highly political environments where there is a lot of emotion and a shortage of decisional data. Here, sourcing capabilities tend to be weak. Articulating a sourcing strategy—or, even simpler, tactical and strategic initiatives in IT—is a great starting point. Some people need this mindset in order to see themselves in a future state of success. How can they make the jump if they don't have a factual illustration? This is an important role of IT leadership.

A common error that occurs in IT organizations new to sourcing is the confusion of internal costs in comparison to proposed pricing from outside partners. **They request proposals for services with SLAs beyond what they are delivering, with requirements for data that their internal toolsets can't provide and then they compare only their wages (void of burden rate) in comparison to external proposal price.** They end up getting a lot less for the same cost, as they tend to keep the services in-house in these instances. We recommend that sourcing evaluations do include internal comparison as a rating. However, pricing should include burden rate and look at all variables, such as those on the evaluation form exampled here. (Note: this can be downloaded from http://www.getoutofit.net.

Service Provider Evaluation

Ability	Vendor A	Vendor B	Internal
Technical Expertise			
Business/IT Process Expertise			
Experience of Key Personnel			
Industry Experience			
Transition Planning/Process			
Transitioning employees, assets and intellectual property			

Track Record	Vendor A	Vendor B	Internal
Corporate Viability			
Reference Checks / Documented Success			
Controls, Governance and Compliance			
Partnerships			
As a place to work			

Customer Focus	Vendor A	Vendor B	Internal
Strategic Vision			
Clear Expectations for Service Levels			
Flexible Reporting			
Flexible Pricing/Costing Models			
Customer Support and Relationship Management			

Agility	Vendor A	Vendor B	Internal
Documented approach to integrating and delivering solutions			
Scalability			
Investment in infrastructure to support commitment to the market			
Willingness to hire your people			
Demonstrated ability to sense change and respond accordingly			

Trust	Vendor A	Vendor B	Internal
Incentives to innovate			
Ability to accept and manage change			
Contract flexibility			
Risk distribution, terms & conditions and cost			
Willingness to collaborate			
Cultural Fit			

Rate on a scale of 1-5 and weight accordingly

Assuming that sourcing is all about saving money is a misperception. Business units are not always thinking about cost savings. They are often thinking about skill set access, time to implementation, future cost avoidance, better decisional data, and toolsets. They are often hoping to get a lot more value for a little more or the same cost.

The most important takeaway from this section is that sourcing is a critical competency. Those who have the acumen to negotiate and govern multi-sourced workforces are in high demand. Some large organizations have even established the position of Chief Sourcing Officer (CSO). Search Google for "Chief Sourcing Officer" and you will be amazed at how real this trend is.

Revenue Generation

What were the revenues of your ITO last year? One of the most admirable traits of leading ITOs is that they impact top-line revenue. Some IT leaders are reestablishing themselves as revenue-generating participants. They have chosen to battle the pure cost-center stigma. Some even have business development or salespeople promoting their wares.

At a basic level, some are marketing their bandwidth and infrastructure to offset their investments. Although I call this basic, it doesn't mean it's common. I am simply referring to the selling of infrastructure components of IT. As a CEO who knows what percent of his budget is allocated to IT, I realize it's a question worth asking. These, too, are important questions: Can I get a return on this investment, even if it is through multi-dimensional relationships? Can it be done so I can cover much of my cost while keeping critical intellectual property? This mindset isn't without its challenges, but these are necessary questions.

At a grander level, some IT organizations have focused so well on meaningful initiatives that outside organizations are paying them for their value propositions (above infrastructure). I call these accomplishments *grander* because their solutions come from value focus. Some IT organization— like Marshfield Clinic, M&I Bank, Mayo Clinic, and Quad/graphics— have innovated so well on behalf of their customers or patients that their competition is paying *them* in order to catch up. Imagine your peer or competitor asking if they can pay you to deploy one of your internally developed solutions!

At Quad/graphics, they have developed divisions called Quad/Tech and QuadData Solutions. Quad/Tech has competitors buying printing solutions from them. This not only generates revenues, but also gives Quad/graphics a competitive advantage because their peers are using their solutions a generation behind them. As discussed in Chapter Four, "Moving in the Right Direction," QuadData has revenues of about $12 million and is helping their clients improve collaboration, individualize collateral, and gain stronger decisional data.

Marshfield Clinic is improving the tracking of child immunizations, distribution of prescriptions, and access of Electronic Health Records. Their IT organization has developed one of the first paperless charting systems in the country, and it is being used system wide. The impact of their IT innovation on patient experience and error reduction makes them the envy of many competitors in their industry. Marshfield has even established an IT commercialization initiative to market their offerings. Prior to that, they had already generated a couple million dollars from their innovations. Their culture of purpose and leadership has prompted wonderful innovation on behalf of their patients.

M&I Bank is committed to improving the world of banking. An offshoot of theirs, Metavante, is now a $1 billion banking-solutions company. Other banks are procuring from them their methods of deploying merchant capture, online bill payment, transaction processing, and more.

Mayo Clinic is so well known for their advances in healthcare that their IT developments sometimes go unnoticed. They have developed many solutions that are in demand and sometimes sold to peers. They have developed an incredibly innovative way of archiving and retrieving PACS images (visit Teramedica.com). Furthermore, they have developed solutions advancing applications for Single Logon, a Biomedical Imaging software tool called Analyze and Lexgrid: A data dictionary tool for establishing standards for medical terminology used in EMR applications.

In many of these innovations, you can find developments that actually get spun off to become "for-profit" companies that are highly successful in their own right.

These are just four brief snapshots of successful value centers. In each company, underlying income and advantage is a culture very much in tune with the delta between *what is* and *what can be* in their industry. They are applying their technical know-how to improve the way they and others in their industry do business.

Some readers are quick to assume that I am a proponent of building solutions instead of purchasing them. I typically am not, nor is the group of contributors to this book. But when there is a need without a solution, I celebrate those who survey the landscape and plan, architect, implement, and manage solutions that the market will buy.

Theoretically it would be great to have an ITO that is a profit center, but it is next to impossible for most companies—even generating revenues is difficult for some. Years of focus on cost reduction, consolidation, and standardization has steered IT cultures away from considering revenue generation. To be successful, most ITOs will have to let go of some of their self-imposed constraints. This represents entrepreneurship at its purest, and there can be both risk and reward. Of the six criteria discussed in this chapter, creating and selling solutions is the most optional. In some cases it is ill-advised. However, if there is a real need that is not being met in the market place, and you can build, deploy and build a profit center off of it, you are worthy of everyone's admiration.

A Solid Asset Management Methodology

IT needs to be run like a business. In business, there always seem to be trendy, buzz-generating initiatives—Total Quality Management (TQM), Learning Organization, Six Sigma, Lean Manufacturing, Lean Office, Knowledge Management, and so forth. In the future there will be new initiatives with new cool names. There are very good reasons for these initiatives, and none will succeed without good information. IT organizations with a solid approach to asset management have information that assists tactical decisions and provides insight into IT's impact on company strategy. Waste elimination (leanness) and agility can improve dramatically with the maturity of IT asset management.

The Mayo Clinic illustrates this well. While some in Mayo Clinic's IT department can identify where they still have room for improvement, they are certainly ahead of the curve from my perspective. They have tools, policies, and procedures to better understand what assets they have, where they exist, and how are they being used. They can improve leanness by eliminating waste such as non-used assets or licenses (which can also be redeployed). They are more agile in rolling-out solutions with significantly less planning time, risk, and resources than other organizations. They can also use this information in vendor negotiations for serious hard-dollar savings.

For Mayo Clinic and others that have a good handle on their assets, their agility is greater. The time it takes to accurately budget is also faster. Risks and errors in implementing new solutions are lower. How long does it take your organization to do OS migrations or roll out applications? Including planning and discovery time, does it take you days or a year? That is the difference between organizations that do it well and those that don't. Because of asset management and product consistency within EED at Mayo, they can have one technician upgrade applications on 2,500 PCs on a Monday morning and have 10,000 done by lunch on Thursday with flexible afternoons and few hiccups.

However, the benefits of asset management go beyond controlling assets and costs. When you incorporate the IT Infrastructure Library (ITIL), you have a consistent approach to IT Service Management. With every company's increasing dependence on IT to satisfy business needs and strategy, there is an increased need for high-quality IT services. Again, this chapter isn't the simple recipe to greatness, but it contains checklist of components of great ITOs. For more information on ITIL asset management, Google "ITIL asset management" and find 888,000+ articles in .10 seconds. If you are an enterprise-sized organization and not in the process of implementing ITIL, you are behind the curve.

Finally, recognize that although it is IT leadership's responsibility to drive success in this area, increasingly they are partnering with outside resources. As desktop lifecycle services are increasing outsourced, this is one of the many benefits. Perhaps these activities are increasingly sourced out because all of the tools to drive good asset management have been purchased many times before, with only poor returns. It takes solid policies and procedures and a long-tenured ownership of the initiative to get to effective results. It is often easier to get asset-management accountability with vendors than internal teams that have previously failed to get real-time results. It doesn't matter whether asset and life-cycle management are done in house or through partnerships, but it is essential that they occur.

Financial and Performance Measurement

If leading ITOs make money, they must have received the money (or time) to invest in the first place. Where does that money come from? Garnering financial support for initiatives used to be easier for IT than it was for other departments because of IT's forward-thinking appeal. Today, IT has to compete for their part of the budget like never before. Almost all ITOs cite that pressures remain strong to contain IT investments. Yet IT still tends to be the largest growth sector within overall departmental budgets.

So which comes first? Today, measurement is a catalyst for additional support. The IT professionals that measure well have two key variables. First, you will find a balanced approach to measuring financial and performance objectives of their investments. Secondly, you will find leadership that follows through on the measurement and marketing of both successes and failures. There is no shortage of organizations with good people and good intent, or even those with good measurement approaches that fail to see through their responsibility of reporting the benefits of IT initiatives.

A good balanced approach will map out important financial measures in the form of cost-benefit analysis, return on investment (ROI), and even profitability in areas of customer-facing innovation. The second, softer side of benefit—performance and productivity measures—are increasingly discounted by some frustrated business leadership. From our perspective, these are still extremely valuable and IT leadership should continue to promote their measures on quality, efficiency, and customer and employee satisfaction.

Producing a balanced scorecard on an IT initiative, or the ITO, as a whole may feel like a daunting task. Some of the best reports, though, have a smaller defined set of measures to ensure that each measurement is both completed and read. In the end, reading these measurements is the objective.

IT measurements are primarily for internal justification and future support. Failure to measure proactively can cause serious consequences if perceptions of the Board and executives (in the absence of good reporting) become their reality. Leading ITOs use measurement as a weapon when competing for future financial support.

Most IT organizations today do a fair job of measuring SLAs and reporting on efficiency gains. The success of financial measurement depends greatly on up-front agreements with business management. As a result, success is measured extremely subjectively. I strongly suggest you meet with business leadership to establish what a winning initiative report looks like. Go into that management discussion prepared with a list of measures that you are looking to assess. Failure to do so will have you leaving with only a ninety-day hard-profit return request.

Marketing Your Successes

If you could rate the complexity of all departmental initiatives and projects in a business today, you would find that IT probably owns the strongest share of responsibility. Why, then, do ITOs do such a poor job of marketing their initiatives and successes? For twenty years I have watched IT teams execute some pretty amazing feats. If lucky, they will take a moment to high-five and celebrate over a beer before moving on to the next project. Most in IT tend to think, "That's life in IT," but should it be that way? Smart IT organizations market themselves wisely. IT professionals that have a hard time promoting accomplishments should step aside and delegate this very important responsibility.

As I toured ITOs at a whirlwind pace over the last year, I asked my contacts, "How do you market your ITO and its impact?" Their response was nearly unanimous: "We don't!" Even organizations that do a great job of measuring value don't take this important step. I only found three real exceptions to this rule—CUNA Mutual Group (CUNA), Harley-Davidson Motor Company, and Intel.

Both CUNA and Intel published impressive annual reports similar to those of publicly-held companies. Rick Roy, the acting Chief Information and Technology Officer (CITO) said, "There are numerous benefits that have resulted from publishing this annual report. First, it establishes credibility within management that we are running our organization as a business. Secondly, it builds trust with other departments. They can see that we care and are committed to the same thing they are. Thirdly, a surprisingly great benefit was that individuals in IT could see how they are impacting organizational outcomes. You would think it is glaringly evident, but it is not for everyone. They can also see that we need to be fiscally responsible in our investments. Finally, it helps in recruiting talent and bringing them up to speed." I find this a fairly eloquent justification for the exercise.

I asked Reid Engstrom, Director of Information Services for Harley-Davidson, if he would be willing to share what he publishes. He sent me an extremely impressive quarterly report. It provided a well-articulated overview of all IS projects. Every single project is mapped to a "Functional Strategy" with its "Strategic Contribution" defined. Other key subheadings in each project's overview were Project Mission Statement, Business Value, ROI, rollout timeline, Business Results, and Project Status. After reviewing the document, I couldn't help wondering how much more financial support an average ITO would have if it went through the rigors of documenting their project overviews in this fashion.

I also picked up on Reid Engstrom's enthusiasm for mistakes or the lack thereof. I asked Reid about his positive demeanor when discussing such challenges. He responded, "I simply see these not as crises, but opportunities to do great things, to make an impact." It made me think of Paul Romer's quote, "A crisis is a terrible thing to waste." I can tell you that I didn't see any evidence of crisis in Harley-Davidson's project overview, but perhaps that's because of the willingness to learn continually that Reid embodies.

If you want to know more about Intel and their annual ITO report, see it for yourself at http://www.intel.com/it/business. You can download reports from previous years and see how their approach to reporting has evolved. Obviously, Intel has a bigger budget than most companies to create this type of collateral. Nevertheless, do not be deterred. This is your opportunity to creatively position your IT group's skills and strategic potential. Here are some suggestions.

For possible resources, consider engaging:
- Vendor cooperative funding and assistance
- Your company's marketing department for assistance.
- An internship through the marketing department of a local college (with creative layout expertise)

Suggestions:
- Think of yourself as the CEO of IT. How do you want to take your IT organization to market?
- Appoint an IT-dedicated marketing/communications professional.
- Brand your projects or give them a theme.
- Publish your successes. Create an IT annual report. Search the Web for great examples of annual reports
- Enter IT award programs and publicize wins with business partners to increase your credibility. Your department probably has the best PMO in the organization, so use it.
- Have an internal award for best project case study; this perpetuates a practice of both measurement and marketing. Internal recognition is also a motivator that stands longer than money.

If successful, your marketing collateral will:
- Establish credibility and understanding within your business leadership
- Help your ITO sees how the things it does translates to value, client experience, market share, strategy, etc.
- Help in recruiting efforts
- Foster a culture of innovation and agility

Imagine that the amount of financial support you get to innovate could be in direct proportion to the amount of marketing you do. As stated before, your content needs to go beyond just the utility aspects of uptime and user satisfaction. These are important, but also map outcomes to business strategy. Get on it!

Leadership

There is no shortage of great leadership books today. If you are looking for general leadership characteristics, I recommend *The 21 Indispensable Qualities of a Leader* by John C. Maxwell (Nelson Business). In the next chapter, I cover the difference between Leaders and Managers and discuss how change must be lead. I will also cover how good leaders solicit ideas and turn them into benefit.

In this chapter, I wanted to make some quick points about leadership in IT. Leadership must happen everywhere within an IT organization. The culture of old-school hierarchy is out and empowerment at every level is in. Obviously, it is my bias that within this culture, concepts shared in this book (i.e., opening of eyes to purpose, strategy, marketplace, and how to innovate) are prevalent. For high-ranking staff, the following leadership behaviors are worthy of mention:

- Encourage IT staff to get out of their cubicles or server closet and communicate in person through out the organization. The era is over where the nerd that doesn't communicate gets to hide. Furthermore, those in IT are encouraged to be the builders of morale throughout the organization.

- In the midst of technical certification training, make available curriculum that helps staff build their business acumen. Career paths in IT have missed this for too long.

- Consider appointing different IT ambassadors to each business unit. IT staff may see the broader role they can play, and it can prompt the development of revenue-generating ideas.

- Follow up and follow through on the measurement and marketing of IT initiatives. There should be accountability to make sure this is done.

- Establish regular meetings for individuals to share and discuss the organization's strategic plan, the current state of affairs, and how IT can help drive success.

- Help IT staff understand the difference between strategic and tactical approaches (the latter of which drive value focus and sourcing strategies).

- Practice solid recruitment and orientation procedures. Get the right people on the team.
- Encourage activities that clarify the human-need purpose of your company's customer.
- Support valuable conferences or affiliations (though not all are).
- Maintain a sincere interest in understanding what the ideal state of IT in your company looks like. Do you provide the best decisional data, a superior client experience, best agility, or implemented best practices?
- Determine if the need to measure performance is blended with the patience to innovate.

Chapter Six: Action Items/Points to Ponder

1) Value Focus and Sourcing Strategy: Assemble a think tank to clearly define in what areas IT must excel in order to drive the company's competitive position. Next, develop a message so staff can succinctly articulate your sourcing strategy. Finally, help staff in tactical positions understand strategic thinking and how it can improve their career path.

2) Revenue Generation: Consider appointing IT staff as ambassadors to various business units. Beyond the role of liaison, they should be chartered with identifying investments that can help generate revenues.

3) Solid Asset Management Methodology: When will you be able to quickly tell what you have, where it is, and how it is being used? Many have heard that success in asset management is 75 percent process, procedure, and accountability; 25 percent toolsets. If you haven't achieved this on your own, the obstacles could be cultural. Asset Management eliminates resource-waste and increases agility. If you can't get there yourself, find a life-cycle management partner to own this facet of your business.

4) Marketing of Successes: Consider appointing someone within IT that can add marketing coordination to their role. The benefit goes beyond creating awareness of IT outside of the department, and it also helps those in IT understand departmental interdependencies and how they impact outcomes. Whoever serves this role can develop partnerships with the internal marketing department, vendors (for case study support), and outside resources to make this happen.

5) Financial and Performance Measurement: These measures are typically for internal justification and understanding. Establish with business leadership what the right scorecard looks like and make accountable its regular completion.

6) Leadership and Culture: Although you need to market the success of your ITO, as an individual you can execute well quietly. Promote your trust and reliance upon others to be great in all things (especially self-education).

NOTES

NOTES

The Best Competitive Advantage

Chapter Seven

Agility n.
Characterized by quickness, lightness, and ease of
movement; nimble.
2. Mentally quick or alert: an agile mind.
          —The American Heritage® Dictionary

Chapter Seven: The Best Competitive Advantage

Hopefully you recognize by now that we all need to take ownership of helping our employer provide the right client experience and compete in its market. Innovating in a competitive company rocks! Once one becomes an innovator, addiction to it is common.

Some individuals get addicted to continually looking for what they can do to create competitive advantage. The addiction reward is, and should be, respect from peers and management for innovation. What a great state to be in! However, all addictions have challenges, and this one is no different. Those who have chosen to be the best them in their industry and innovate as such, are realizing that any competitive advantage coming from individuals or IT by itself is increasingly short lived. In this flattened world, any advantages gained are quickly countered by competition that has a similar access to resources. The need to innovate is constant. In fact, your organization's only long-term competitive advantage is its ability to recreate itself faster than the competition.

Now all of the lessons of this book up until now have been focused on helping you grow and innovate as an individual. Do not let the short life span of competitive advantages coming from individual or IT contributions dissuade you from pursuing them. Your competitors won't, and all of my efforts thus far would be in vain. I simply want you to recognize that innovating in a vacuum today typically yields short-term advantages. It's a great place to start, but the innovation junkies soon realize that fostering a culture of innovation and agility is the ultimate state.

Imagine that your organization can react to changes in your industry more efficiently and effectively than the competition. Imagine that your organization can get ideas to market faster than the competition. This type of agility is vital if an organization wants to attain or maintain market leadership.

Technology Doesn't Change That Much!

While this book is not about my company PDS, sharing the company's history is one of the best ways I know to illustrate what business agility is. I think you will also take away that without agility, a company's death is in time certain. While being recognized multiple times as one of the fastest growing companies and one of the best companies to work for; the real accomplishment is that it was conducted through multiple business model changes. Also later in this chapter, I will discuss some components of culture and approach we used to aid us in this accomplishment. This certainly is not the only recipe, nor is it an "I did it my way" story. It has often times felt more like survival than success over the last 20 years. Lets the story begin:

Like many entrepreneurial companies, Memory and More Ltd (M&M) had humble beginnings. In a basement office, four friends threw in their loose change to become equal owners. M&M offered memory chips for PC upgrades and targeted as computer resellers. We opened our doors in 1986, when the computer industry was relatively young. The "More" from M&M was if you ever received faulty memory from us, you would have your replacements cross-shipped overnight at M&M's expense. This was a differentiator, as most memory brokers were short on trust in an era of fly-by-night resellers.

Business was great out of the gate. In the first full year, the company did $1.8 million in revenues, followed by $2.4 million the next year. Then things began to change. The cost of entry became so low that hundreds of memory brokers popped up. Margins became so thin that the survivability of any vendor was very much in question, and the memory market became known as the "whore market."

If we can call the start of the company the first creation, the second creation came when M&M leadership decided the company would become a computer component wholesaler. With channel relationships in place, why not distribute all of the parts that make up the computer? It worked, and the business grew in the newly diversified model. M&M was shipping multifunction cards, floppy drives, hard drives, and more to resellers in many states. Then things began to change, again! Huge consolidation occurred among component wholesalers in the late 1980s and early 1990s, with primarily two (from two hundred) remaining today: Tech Data and Ingram Micro. All of M&Ms reseller clients could now buy their components for the same prices as M&M. Again, margins were thin and survivability was in question.

The third iteration of M&M happened with a decision to assemble all of the components into PCs and establish a reseller program. M&M would go to mom & pop computer shops east of the Mississippi and provide training, parts closets, warranty reimbursement, and cooperative marketing dollars. It had all the look and feel of a Tier 1 reseller program. It worked! In 1992, M&M was a computer manufacturer and distributor to six hundred resellers around the country. Once again, things began to change. The strategy used by computer companies to take market share away from IBM in the 1980s began to backfire. Competitors would take the cover off of the computer and say, "See, it's not IBM, its Intel. All computers are the same. Hence, buy on price." It worked, and IBM lost market share. Now, however, consumers developed an even-keel perception of PCs and abandoned mom & pop computer shops for mass resellers. In 1993, two hundred resellers remained on M&M's customer list. Despite aggressive offensive efforts in 1994, that number dwindled down to thirty-eight by the fourth quarter. Survivability became in question once again.

In 1995, M&M abandoned its client base and opened a direct PC purchase program. The M&M name was changed to Paragon Development Systems, Inc., which was the name of the PCs being sold. The fourth iteration of the company focused on large enterprise accounts, because M&M could keep a similar approach to that of resellers. We could provide product training, parts closets, and warranty reimbursements so that enterprise organizations could be self-maintainers. This was very popular in the late 1990s and the company quadrupled in size over the next four years. Things couldn't be better. As always, things began to change One hundred percent of the revenues were coming from PC sales. Y2K had been very good for the company because so many of our customers replaced all of their PCs. In 1999 PDS's customers breathed a collective sigh of relief, as all their new PCs would avoid the perceived risks of Y2K and that they wouldn't have to buy more units anytime soon.

Similar to IBM, PDS now needed to move from being a "hardware" company to a "services" company. It was a major cultural shift which required leadership at all levels. Although PDS remained a great source for IT products, it spent much of its time helping IT organizations of large enterprise companies improve management of their lifecycles. As with the previous four iterations, PDS managed its consistent track record of growth through the fifth business model recreation. It did help, however, that an acquisition of Entre's occurred. As you might have guessed, things began to change. In the beginning of 2003, PDS clients started to say, "Stop showing us how to manage our IT asset lifecycles and do it for us instead!"

A sixth business model needed to be born. To add to its business model of helping IT organizations conduct their business better, PDS would need to invest millions of dollars to become an **outsourcing option** to its clients and prospects. Today, that is where it stands for now. PDS architects, supplies, implements and manages its clients' IT.

Here is an important point: This story is not about PDS! Sure, I have fleeting moments of pride when I think about nineteen consecutive years of growth. I am certainly proud of the PDS team that has yielded distinctive competitive advantages. This is not the story either. The example here demonstrates that all competitive advantages other than agility are static and will fade. Certainly most industries are not as dynamic as IT, but the fact remains: The only long-term competitive advantage is agility. This is the fundamental ability to recreate yourself faster than the competition.

People often say to me, "Oh, you're in IT? You must see a lot of change." They are typically referring to changes in technology. This makes me smile and I respond that technology change is trivial. We eat technology change for breakfast. The transformational changing of business models is the real challenge in today's global marketplace. PDS would be gone if it was refining itself tactically to be a better chip broker, component wholesaler, or PC distributor. Fortunately, all of this was done in a culture to win, versus one simply to avoid dying. Changes were anticipated ahead of time, allowing PDS to evolve quickly enough to keep its growth record intact. Such change is not easy, but can be exhilarating if you choose to approach it the right way.

So beyond playing to win and innovating individually, I want to encourage you to recognize that the best advantage you can yield is a fostering of a culture that is agile. Everything is changing. Consumers don't want to be seen as consumers, but as individuals who want to interact their desired way. Increasing competition, evolving regulations, market demand, and recruiting talent all require that businesses build an agile culture. Although the culture of agility is fostered more than created, there are some components you can look to incorporate into your organization.

Components of the Agile Organization

Many variables make an organization agile. Through my experiences at PDS and on my tours of various businesses, I have identified three of the most important qualities. Extremely agile organizations have informed employees, more leadership than management, and, of course, the ability to capture input.

> *All is connected ... no one thing can change by itself.*
> —*Paul Hawken*

The Informed Employee

Agility requires informed employees. Developing employees that embrace and celebrate change requires leadership and information. Different employees in an organization learn and grow different ways. Using various methods, agile organizations spend more time informing their employees about the necessary elements everyone must understand:

The customer's voice: Hearing the customer's voice and understanding their desires is a great catalyst to push development and projects through the organization. I have seen individuals militantly defend why they do something before visiting and listening to a customer. Then, miraculously, they were more open and innovative. Agile organizations encourage HR and leadership to look for ways to share their clients' voices and demands. They inform their colleagues what the customer is seeking. I use "customer" instead of "the customers" here because in the era of individual, mass approaches to marketing, production and distribution are decreasingly enough.

The company values: Perhaps as important as a mission statement is a clear and widely-shared message about the company's values, strategic direction, and urgency of its purpose. Culture statements are used in recruiting and adhered to by leadership. Components of grace over guilt, purpose over duty, and empowerment vs. bureaucracy are key to innovation and agility. There should be a specific component of innovation in the shared message as well. Certainly, performance is a critical value. However, making and selling the current offering isn't secondary to the innovation. It is a "one and the other" instead of an "either/or" decision. Balance the need for performance and commitment with the patience to innovate and you have will attract and retain great people

The corporate strategy: Most IT professionals have heard the axiom that the value of IT is in direct proportion to the alignment of its application to the strategy of the company. That holds true for all departments and divisions. The value of departments like HR, finance, training, and administration goes up with their alignment to the business's goals. Therefore, it is a given that the truly informed employee understands how they contribute to its success. At PDS, we have found that teaching individuals how to do something is not enough. They should understand why the task is important and its interdependencies with other parts of the organization. Sustainable success is in direct proportion to the percentage of staff driving strategy.

The forces of change: It is hard to motivate a workforce, especially one comprised of young workers, to change without explaining the purpose. Challenges to the status quo (i.e., client expectations, market changes, competitive pressures, regulatory compliance, or new infrastructure) must be succinctly framed and articulated. Without this, change and innovation is slow. I also think that the most successful organizations have forums to deliver these messages in person. Few people can convey tone of voice in an e-mail, and the forces of change should be explained with both sympathy and urgency.

Information is not only for business leadership, but for everyone. Agility requires everyone to be able to shift priorities or adjust behavior based on information. All employees should have access to data on their daily performance. Informing employees includes identifying critical success indicators that need to be monitored, as well as a ranking of which indicators are most successful. You get what you measure, so measure what you want to get.

Leadership and learning are indispensable to each other.
—John F. Kennedy

Information and learning are so important to agility that many organizations today are appointing Chief Learning Officers (CLOs). I was browsing the May 2005 issue of *Chief Learning Officer* magazine and saw a graphic that did a good job of depicting the value of real-time learning and information access versus the old-school approach of orientation training and then continual learning by mistake. The article was written by Frank J. Anderson Jr. (*Chief Learning Officer*'s 2004 CLO of the Year) and Christopher R. Hardy, Ph.D., the learning architect and strategic planner for the Defense Acquisition University. They granted me permission to share their views and graphic on the importance of learning in an agile environment.

The Bottom Line

The real value of an agile learning environment is portrayed in the following graphic. With integration, speed, reach, and agility, workforce performance can rapidly grow. Without it, new knowledge will decay quickly after training and cannot easily be renewed.

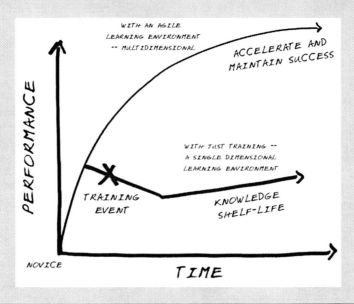

As we look to the future, learning leaders will continue to extend the speed and reach of learning assets by deploying smart business tools, workflow learning assets, and search technologies, and will be even more connected to their workforces. Learning transformation will continue, and corporate universities will play a pivotal role in any envisioned agile learning environment. All learning assets must be designed to reach the extended enterprise: Customers, suppliers, partners, and shareholders should all have access. Additionally, with a multidimensional approach and learning strategy, employees, customers, suppliers, partners, and shareholders can remain connected through the knowledge-sharing framework. Thus, when thoughtfully deployed, a multidimensional approach provides the right amount of content when and where needed. The integration, real-time access to expertise and knowledge, and ubiquitous connectivity of learning assets, set in motion a huge paradigm shift from the traditional classroom environment of the 20th century to the total learning environment of the 21st century.

More Leadership than Management

Change must be led not managed! Now one could take offense to my statement that "agility requires more leadership than management." However, I do not believe people are hardwired. Individuals may lean toward one more than the other, but can also choose to change hats when needed. I will explain the differences between managers and leaders in a moment, but let first emphasize that leaders are not just people of title. Agile organizations need leadership everywhere. Educating an opinion leader that is low on hierarchy can have a huge impact on the rate and adoption of change. Every time PDS has faced real change, we find ourselves educating good prospective leaders at all levels (and bringing on new talent with the leadership tendency). In times of normalization, where we are trying either to do more of the same thing or the same thing better, we get into management mode. Below is an organizational change scale:

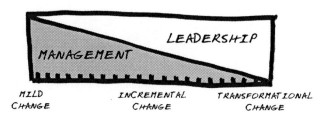

The Organizational Change Scale

Grab a pen and mark on the above scale what level of change is needed to get your organization to its desired outcome. Look up and you can see what representation of leadership is needed to get you there. This sums up what I learned from our previous business model changes. *In times of stability (doing more of the same, or same thing better), management is key. If the desired future for the organization is different (i.e., new market, model, value propositions, etc.), you need a stronger mix of leadership.*

This scale shows that organizations always need a blend of both. I am not suggesting that one is better than the other. *If you have leadership without management, you have chaos. In times of major change, management without leadership can prompt anarchy and attrition.* Both management and leadership are very important. Individuals just need to be encouraged to shift their tendencies based on the level of change that the organization is facing.

What's the difference between management and leadership?

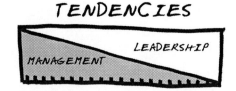

MANAGEMENT VS. LEADERSHIP

- PROCESS
- DUTY
- TACTICAL
- DO THINGS RIGHT
- PLAY NOT TO LOSE

- PEOPLE
- PURPOSE
- STRATEGIC
- DO THE RIGHT THING
- PLAY TO WIN

Obviously, people tend to resist change. I promote leadership over management in high change. High change requires strategic planning, communication, and proper execution of goals. It is different than doing more of the same thing or the same thing better. Good leadership can paint a picture of the desired outcome at a future date and work backwards to show what is needed to get there.

Those with a management tendency have a habit of looking tactically from where they are, determining what the team can do to improve what they are currently doing (see illustration). The outcome may differ greatly for those who adopt strategic leadership tendencies.

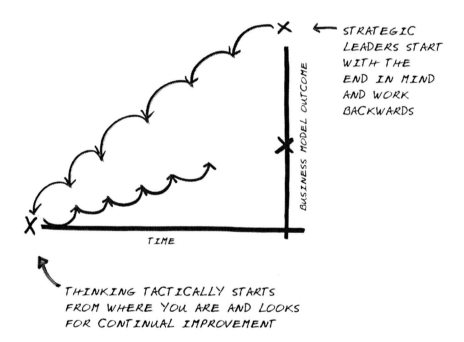

I emphasize leadership over management in this chapter because we are talking about agility. This is about your entire organization's ability to adapt to changes faster than its competition. For some companies, it may be about getting new products to market faster. Regardless, employees will resist change if leadership isn't both sympathetic and educational on the purpose of that change.

The Ability to Capture Input

Imagine right now that someone within your organization has a truly great idea for a new value proposition. Is it easy to submit this idea? Is there a commonly understood repository for ideas? Is there a methodology to turn that idea into benefit?

An agile organization needs more than informed and innovative individuals. Without the ability to get ideas to market promptly, what advantage have you gained? Without the efficient ability to incorporate lessons-learned into your offering or organization, you will lose the desired advantage. Without good methods for idea capture, an organization's return on their talented individuals is diminished. How long does it take you to define, refine, define, and refine your new approach to serving the customer? Getting a return on ideas is something that I could easily dedicate a whole book to. I will summarize some suggestions as succinctly as possible. You have to have a methodology for:

- Soliciting input from employees, clients, prospects, and vendors
- Capturing, classifying, and developing input
- Turning input into a benefit
- Measuring success
- Recognizing and rewarding contributors

Soliciting input

Basic Solicitation—It was an awfully wonderful event in my life. I was working in extremely disorganized factory one summer between college semesters. After I offered some suggestions on how we could reorganize the shop floor to drive efficiency, I was told, "You are not paid to think." That's where the awful part came—it was a sock in the gut. But wonderfully, it was the catalyst for success in my organization. We constantly ask employees, customers, and vendors, **"What should we start, stop, or think about doing?"** Sometimes I qualify the question by adding at the end, "… to drive cost reduction, productivity improvement, time-to-market, or better client experience.

Here's the bottom line: when that question gets asked multiple times, people begin to continually answer the question even when it is not getting asked. I encourage all leaders to be humble enough to constantly ask this question. Encouraging colleagues to share start, stop or think about direction also fosters ownership because you are showing that you are dependent on them, not the other way around. This is the most basic of inputs, but characterizing your culture in this way helps tremendously. There is no question that organizations following the historical buzz of Corporate America (Total Quality Management, Learning Organization, Lean Management, Mass Customization, Six Sigma, etc.) have the easiest time getting to agility. This is because ownership and measurement are now in the culture.

Specific Solicitation—There are many ways to automate "the suggestion box". One very simple approach is to designate an e-mail address in your company's distribution list for ideas. You can have multiple hoppers for ideas that fall within differing classifications. There could be repositories for suggestions improving client experience, operations, products, and service offerings. Just make sure that each hopper has an owner.

Using PDS as an example, so much of our innovation and collaborations happens today within a SharePoint culture. However, the simplicity of the e-mail repository has been very effective. At PDS, we have a Quality e-mail address for corrective and preventative action. We have a KM (Knowledge Management) e-mail for refining our approaches or offerings. We have a Business Development e-mail address for new ideas or offerings. Each one of these addresses is governed by a methodical way of responding promptly to the contributor so they know that their suggestion has not fallen on deaf ears.

Beyond having an individual owner responding to the contributor, PDS also has teams with methodologies to turn such ideas into a benefits (or outcome responses). We will identify different types of categorizations in a moment. The point here is that if you don't have distribution mailboxes like this, consider it. It has helped us at PDS, because it removes the obstacle to contribute/collaborate. This helps tremendously as long as you do the following: First, have an owner of the address that has authority to get things done or requisition resources. Secondly, you must provide feedback to the contributors so they see that input isn't going into the abyss. There is no question that there is a cost to responding to all ideas, even bad ones, but without this employees may have a negative attitude towards providing input.

Finally, the organization needs to know that input isn't "tattling." Corporate meetings need to reinforce the benefits that have come from input (and reward contributors) by citing factual illustrations.

> *The measure of success is not whether you have a tough problem to deal with, but whether it is the same problem you had last year.*
> —John Foster Dulles, former Secretary of State

The most common means of idea solicitation is specific "brainstorming sessions," collaboration cafés, or team "pow-wows" to solve a current challenge. Small groups with short timeframes can solve big problems.

I recall an event that drove a different type of thinking in our culture. I was at a leadership retreat where our facilitator asked a group of twenty employees to identify the main challenges facing our company. We prioritized them and had five groups of four people solve five major problems in just seven minutes. It was amazing; when you only have seven minutes, you don't spend time justifying current or past decisions. You skip history, cut through bureaucracy, and outline the path to the desired state. Try it, you will be surprised.

However, recognize these were small groups of only four members—"God so loved the world, he did not send a committee." Sometimes, small groups given authority are more effective. The more time given to solve a problem, the more time it will take to have a solution. Lemke's Corollary posits that, "Work fills the expansive time allotted for its completion." Of course you have to assign ownership with authority to execute it, but you will find a lean approach that cuts through and accomplish the objective.

There are so many forums you can use for gather input that this list could go on indefinitely. These are just some fundamental approaches to drive the behavior of idea contribution.

Data Solicitation—An Agile Organization responds quickly to business changes while fighting off health threats. Identify what good *decisional data* is and focus IT resources on obtaining it. As stated earlier, many companies no longer in existence had an "always-on" infrastructure with happy users. Fill in the blank: We would be advantaged if we knew _____? Ask your CEO or business leadership to fill in the blank if need be. Then apply IT to make that information readily available. I know that this is so basic, but it is the minority that do this well. It is also sometimes good to go back to the basics.

Example of how PDS classifies and capture input

At PDS, we wanted a simple way for everyone to contribute input. At orientation, employees and customers are educated on how we both learn from mistakes and get new ideas to market. This may not be the right way for your organization. The difference between good and great here depends on the size and complexity of the organization, and what dedicated resources can be allocated to each.

In the event that an employee misdirects their input to an undesired channel, the owners of those input channels collaborate and sort misguided input out between them (instead of redirecting the contributor). This eliminates resistance to contribution. Whether you want classified funnels or one big funnel with a designated sorter, every organization should have a common language around the different types of input. People need to know that their help is needed to:

- Improve client experience
- Reduce cost/eliminate waste.
- Improve productivity and operations.
- Improve existing offering and delivery
- Generate new business offerings.
- Make a judgment call and be empowered if a situation arises

Depending on the size of an organization and the number of designated input owners that can be allocated, the number of hoppers may vary. For us there are three:

KM Hopper—Earlier in this chapter, I shared the importance of multi-dimensional learning in agile organizations. We are using the Knowledge Management (KM) hopper KM@pdspc.com to deposit lessons learned for customer-facing activities. Lessons on sales approaches, Project Management Office (PMO), and implementation are deposited regularly. As with all hoppers, someone must take ownership. In this case, the director of Knowledge Management insures that we are learning in as close to real time as possible. What matters is that you have "the business practices, processes, and disciplines that get the right information, in the right place, at the right time so your colleagues can do the task at hand" (Tom Moerke). Organizations that fail to hold in high regard how they are using their collective knowledge to create repeatable, reliable solutions while cutting waste will fail to reach agility. We are using this to improve the rate at which we can dock on clients and make them loyal.

CPAR Hopper—CPAR stands for *c*orrective/*p*reventative *a*ction *r*eport. Organizational errors or inefficiencies are reported here. People can e-mail quality@pdspc.com and the quality director takes action. There is also a cross-functional list of organizational players that are on the quality distribution list so they can provide input promptly. Culturally, you need to promote that reporting errors isn't tattling. Overall, this has been a huge learning tool that has driven operational excellence.

PDS INPUT HOPPERS

BDC Hopper—On the right side of the above image, we have our Business Development (BDC) hopper. If anyone inside or outside of the organization has an idea on new offerings that we should consider taking to market, those get channeled here. The director of Business Development exposes ideas to a Business Development Committee (BDC) to acknowledge and allocate (or not) resources that can be used to move it down further. This team needs to have a strong understanding of both creativity and business process to be successful. If an idea is moved down further, someone will be assigned responsibility to do adequate research on the prospective initiative. Once these findings (success potential, competitive landscape, and industry maturation) are presented to the

BDC, they will determine if it is a go, if it is viable idea to partner with someone, or if it is simply a no-go. If it is determined that it is a go, a short-term competency council (CC)—another cross-functional team—will be built to determine everything required internally and externally to take the new value proposition to market. This group determines how and when we will measure success or failure.

Above all, hoppers exist to create empowerment: People are empowered to do the right things at all times. They need not wait for a hopper response in urgent situation. The hopper may simply take right actions and make them repeatable and reliable. Empowerment runs high and bureaucracy is hated in very agile organizations. With this mindset comes the responsibility to celebrate mistakes learned from. Certainly, the best leaders know how to help the organization learn without throwing the instigator of the mistake under the bus.

Recognition and Rewards

The final "agility component" I want to recognize is recognition and reward. Agile organizations understand that recognition and reward programs are critical to their success. Identify what behavior or actions are to be celebrated and develop a program to do just that. And though you may have a committee of individuals map out the recognition and rewards program, it should be set up that everyone (not just executives) has the ability to publicly recognize anyone, anytime. You can build a program that drives behavior while bolstering belief that their knowledge is paramount. It's the truth, so why not?

At PDS we have a "Kudos" program and dozens are given out weekly. Anyone can send an e-mail to the Kudos address sharing specific information about the behavior that is being appreciated of another. This way, people are recognized as close to their positive action as possible. Recipients get a kudos bar, while their manager and the weekly newsletter get informed. At the end of the year, major recognition awards take this daily behavior into consideration.

Finally, recognition is intentionally placed before reward here. I have found that recognition can be a powerful motivator that oftentimes has more standing power than a monetary reward over time. Either way, these programs are appreciated by employees, so it's important to have a structured approach to them. I was reading an article that did a great job of articulating the approach to rewarding innovation by Paige Leavitt and the American Productivity and Quality Center (APQC).

Rewarding Innovation, by Paige Leavitt

Asking employees to be innovative may seem easy enough. But fostering a creative environment and leveraging valuable ideas that result in viable new products and processes have proven to be quite a challenge. So what can help?

To drive innovation, organizations must determine what works in an innovation context. How do behavior, motivation, appreciation, social cohesion and allegiance, engagement and commitment, and attitudes and feelings come into play? And how can structured rewards and recognition encourage employees to change their behavior?

The American Productivity & Quality Center (APQC) has found that to drive innovation in products and services, an organization needs innovative approaches to rewards and recognition. Given that employees have valid needs for achievement, status, and affiliation, organizations are tasked with providing structure and consistency that will motivate employees to pursue creative and effective ideas.

In working with APQC member companies and generating research for the upcoming Best-Practice Report Using Knowledge Management to Drive Innovation, APQC has found compelling examples of rewards and recognition from historically innovative organizations. The following examples, along with the expert opinion of APQC KM specialist Kimberly Lopez, can serve as a starting point for creating an environment that encourages innovation. "It requires a blending of creativity with business processes to ensure good ideas become of value to the company," said Lopez. "Supporting a creative environment requires innovation to be recognized, nurtured, and rewarded."

The Basics—Those leading organizations that drive innovation through rewards and recognition first addressed the basic principles of encouraging specific behaviors.

- Create a design team.
- Consistently acknowledge those who contribute ideas, knowledge, and time. Senior management may recognize innovative design teams and champions, whereas peers typically nominate and recognize teammates for their contributions to the overall effort.
- Provide special recognition to volunteers, change agents, and model innovators. Keep names associated with contributions.
- Disseminate success stories concerning invention of a successful new product or approach.
- Make innovation self-rewarding. Being perceived as an expert by peers and management matters.
- Link innovation to the core cultural values of the organization. Explain the justification behind rewards and how meeting goals will affect overall and individual outcomes.
- Compile a committee of human resources, knowledge management, research and development, and representatives from business units to develop guidelines and suggestions to encourage innovation.

"Organizations typically have experience encouraging certain productive behaviors," said Lopez. "Many of those lessons learned can be the foundation to encourage innovation from employees."

Design Issues—As with all organizational rewards and recognition, balancing intrinsic and extrinsic motivation is a challenge. *Intrinsic motivation* refers to an internal desire to act, such as when the task itself seems rewarding and meets a person's goals. Extrinsic motivation refers to external encouragement to act in order to meet a final reward. "In recent studies at APQC, best-practice organizations were more likely to explicitly attempt to motivate for innovation," said Lopez. When an organization establishes extrinsic rewards for innovation, it must be wary of

- Attributing more importance to money than it actually has.
- Confusing compensation with rewards.

- Stifling teamwork through individual recognition.
- Ignoring the underlying issues behind behaviors.
- A reward's decreased effectiveness over time.

To instill intrinsic motivation, several innovative organizations have encouraged peer recognition, arranged events, and established work structures conducive to cultivating relevant innovations.

Yet establishing a structure for rewards and recognition involves more than just following a list of guidelines and principles. Challenges lie in ensuring consistency across an organization, yet recognizing the needs of different business units. For instance, innovative sales approaches obviously are separate from innovative manufacturing activities. As a result, best-practice organizations develop guidelines instead of an imposing corporate wide approach.

Organizations must also thoroughly flesh out the structure to administer the reward system: Who decides who gets recognized? How are innovations defined? In addition to innovators, should enablers be rewarded? For each question, there is a delicate balance of pros and cons. For example, it may seem appropriate to let supervisors determine who should be rewarded. After all, they see who commits effort. But this may encourage employees to conceal problems from the persons who could help them. "When supervisors hold control of rewards, employees are less likely to discuss or share failures that can stifle innovation or important lessons," said Lopez. "Don't establish a reward system that will create a fear of failure within the organization."

Organizations are also tasked with determining how much emphasis should be placed on recognizing innovative behavior instead of results. Boeing Rocketdyne has faced issues from recognizing and rewarding the successes of employees. The company has several programs to reward innovative employees, including its Leading Edge award, the Pillar award, and the Engineer of the Year award. Furthermore, an innovator could also be promoted. But the result of recognizing individuals is that cooperation is avoided and knowledge may be hoarded.

At Boeing Rocketdyne, there is a growing belief that innovation comes from an intrinsic sense of motivation and that a reliance on external motivation can stifle cooperation. "An organization cannot create a climate for innovation and knowledge sharing without finding a balance between intrinsic and extrinsic motivators for its employees," said Lopez. "If intrinsic motivation declines, it will take more and more extrinsic rewards to maintain the behavior. And competition for rewards may negatively impact teamwork."

Some organizations have found that recognizing individual achievement is critical for them. Especially when a project involves an extended time frame, recognizing and encouraging innovative behavior must come well before revenue is realized. Organizations operating under the mantra that justice delayed is justice denied often create a close proximity between behavior and rewards. "For best-practice organizations such as NASA and Millennium Pharmaceuticals, a project, whether it is space exploration or taking a drug to market, can occur over decades. It is important for these organizations to recognize their experts at the time of the accomplishment."

Peer Recognition—APQC has found at many historically innovative organizations that extrinsic rewards can actually impede innovation. "As extrinsic motivation—or the perception by the person that they are acting because of extrinsic motivation—increases, intrinsic motivation can decline," said Lopez. "Additionally, focusing on monetary rewards as extrinsic motivators can add further complications. Issues arise when you attribute more importance to money than it actually has and make money more prominent than it needs to be."

Instead of monetary rewards for innovators, 3M relies primarily on peer recognition to encourage innovation. Like Boeing Rocketdyne, 3M wants to avoid employees hoarding of new ideas and failing to collaborate. Instead, 3M employees share ideas for peer recognition. This recognition includes the Technical Circle of Excellence award in which innovators, selected by coworkers, receive a trip to the company retreat in Minnesota. For technical promotions, the ability of somebody to work with others inside and outside their laboratory is very much a part of the promotion criteria, especially at the higher levels. "In addition to peer recognition, 3M celebrates success stories and propagates tales of innovation and contribution," said Lopez. "The stories about great inventors, such as Art Fry, become legends at 3M."

Formal Events—"Bringing people together who would not normally meet is a great way to foster connections that can lead to innovation," said APQC president, Carla O'Dell. To inspire innovation, the World Bank holds programs called "knowledge fairs" as learning opportunities. "The knowledge fairs provide an opportunity to create relationships that build social capital across projects, disciplines, time, and geography," said Lopez. A fair called the Development Marketplace, for instance, provides a venue to seek new ways of addressing poverty. This fair holds a competition—which was initially only between staff and is now open to anyone—to develop innovative ways to fight poverty. In 2002 the competition resulted in 2,400 entries with 204 finalists, and more than 40 of the suggested programs were funded.

The World Bank also uses extrinsic incentives to foster innovation. The innovation and development marketplaces reward outstanding creativity (of both staff and other organizations) in addressing poverty. From these extrinsic rewards to generating enthusiasm through knowledge fairs, the World Bank has patiently shifted the culture to understand that innovation is as important as other work.

Work Structure—At innovative organizations, APQC has found that time must be established for innovation. If employees feel they have to take time away from ostensibly more important work, they won't. "Contrary to popular belief, people do not always work best under pressure and need time to reflect," said Lopez. "In addition to senior management, it is critical that direct supervisors are supportive of such a work structure."

At 3M, laboratory employees operate under a "fifteen-percent rule." The company allows employees to spend fifteen percent of their time on any idea that could benefit 3M. This time is not tracked, but the rule is embedded in the culture; it is seen as a symbol of the freedom and encouragement to generate and develop new ideas, rather than an entitlement of time. 3M supervisors are instructed to respect the concept.

3M also supports innovation with small grants. Both of these programs represent a second chance to fund a project if an idea is not originally approved for development. The two programs represent approximately $1 million out of the total $1.1 billion budget for research and development.

An Innovative Culture—Ultimately, approaches such as formal events, peer recognition, and embedding innovation in a work-structure innovation lead to a dynamic cultural shift: innovation is aligned with the overall goals of the organization. Rewards and recognition, specifically balancing extrinsic and intrinsic incentives, influence how employees approach their responsibilities. "With encouragement and a clear explanation of innovation's place in daily activities, organizations can prosper from their most important resources: their employees," said Lopez.

Chapter Conclusion

I remember reading a US Department of Commerce article in 1987 which surveyed top US and Japanese management to find out what they thought was the best competitive advantage in the year 2000. After getting schooled by Japan's quality systems for the previous 7 years, the majority of US management replied "Quality". Less than a third of Japan's management thought quality was a factor, it was to be a given. The majority of Japanese leaders responded agility. I didn't get it. Since then, I have since spent 20 years in an organization that has had to recreate itself every three years or go away. Now I get it!

While creating this chapter, I should share that I was continually stopping with a sense of … what the hell am I doing … each one of these components is a book by itself. It is my hope that all readers understand that I am not trying to give the complete recipe for an agile organization, simply some example ingredients PDS and other successful companies have used. You may use whatever approach is best suited to inform employees, lead your organization and turn ideas into a benefit. It is just important to understand that the ability to recreate yourself faster than the competition is the only long term advantage. To the junkies addicted to creating distinctive competitive advantages, know that agility is the only one that has standing power.

Chapter Seven: Action Items/Points to Ponder

1) On a scale of 1–10 (10 being the highest), how would you rate
- The agility of your employer? _____
- Your ability to respond to changes in marketplace, regulations, competitive pressures? _____
- The efficiency with which you get new offerings to market? _____

Now, list five things you can do to help your organization improve these ratings:

_____

_____

_____

_____

2) As a catalyst for innovation, identify ways for your IT organization to see and hear the customer in person. (Consider a panel discussion of customers/prospects in front of the ITO, with participants sharing what it would take to make them loyal.)

_____

_____

3) Beyond a mission statement, does your employer have a culture statement or credo? How openly is it visible in your work area? Wall-mounting published values of performance, innovation, empowerment, and grace do make a difference. People should be recruited to this, and leadership should adhere to it.

4) As a team, has the ITO reviewed your company's strategic plan? Have you painted a graphical picture of the end of the strategic plan and worked backwards? Remember to set specific, time-oriented targets (such as the manifestation of excellence in six months, twelve months, eighteen months, and so on).

5) Compared to other industries and organizations, what is the continuing level of change facing your organization? By looking at the change scale, is there a need for more management or leadership training in your organization? What is the best way for you to suggest a solution?

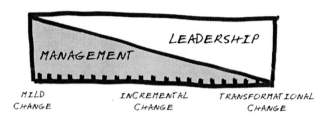

6) How hard would it be to name a particular meeting space as "innovation space" in your workplace? Although preferable, it doesn't need to belong solely to your department. Creating a war room against status quo (and positioning it near an executive sponsor) is a catalyst for good outcomes.

7) On a scale of 1–10 (10 being the highest), how would you rate the clarity of understanding within your department of how to provide input for continuous improvement, or for new value propositions? If needed, how might you suggest improvements for departmental clarification? _____

8) On a scale of 1–10 (10 being the highest), how would you rate the clarity of understanding within your department of how suggestions are processed, developed, and turned into benefits? If needed, how might you suggest improvements for departmental clarification? _____

9) Agile organizations understand the value of information and knowledge management. Does the workforce of your company have the right information in the right place at the right time to do the tasks at hand? How can you use your role in IT to positively impact this objective?

_____

_____

10) Does your employer or department have a recognition and rewards program? Does it drive the necessary behavior that make up an agile organization? Can anyone recognize anyone at anytime? If not, establish a time-bound goal to engage HR to help develop one. It does matter.

NOTES

NOTES

Closing Remarks

Now that you're out, move forward

Get Out of IT While You Can began as a keynote speech for the PDS Technology Conference in 2005. Through numerous retellings to more than a thousand individuals the feedback has been overwhelmingly positive and a validation of the need for this message.

I hope the reasons for publishing this message are evident. The research completed in 2005 validated an assumption I had from years of observing individuals in IT perform their day-to-day functions. The IT professionals who do not see themselves as being *in* IT tend to be happier (the research suggested 22% happier). Beyond being happier, these same individuals exist in a more purposeful, innovative and opportunistic career. If the secret to this existence is simply a choice, then why not start your new life today?

Are you trying to be the best **you** every day? How about the best **you** in your industry? Are you digging a ditch or building a hospital? We in IT have heard countless times that the value of IT is in direct proportion to its application to the business strategy. Why then is it that I find so few in IT who have actually read their employers' strategic plan? My hope is that by simply laying out some exercises, people will read their employers' strategic plan, study best-practices from market leaders and remain cognizant of the competitive landscape. The fact that you have made it through this book suggests that you are more likely to choose excellence over mediocrity and complacency.

Will you choose to get past fear of failure and commit to developing a heightened level of business acumen? Think of the exercises in this book as a mini-MBA course and establish a time-bound goal to do these. The first four chapters might seem basic, but sometimes it is good to go back to the basics. How about a chapter a week? The first five chapter exercises in the next three months? Whatever you decide, just choose to commit! Write down the goal and tape it on your computer monitor (what will you accomplish by what date?). You can do these with a peer, or group and discuss. Also, find exercises (and provide feedback) on getoutofit.net.

Do you see yourself as innovative? Even if it isn't in your job description, can you improve your company's customer experience and loyalty? Can you provide better decisional data which can will help Management and Sales be more effective? When asking questions or offering suggestions across departmental lines, will you refuse to get shy after being bitten once? All too often we see ourselves as being less creative as we age. Choose to that eliminate that perception.

Do you see yourself as collaborative? Are you interested in building an innovative and agile organization that can get products and solutions to market faster than the competition? Can you react to changes in the marketplace faster? Build better business models faster? Even simpler yet, can you have a group discussion to define what is strategic and tactical in you IT organization? There are many very good CIOs who stress the importance of focusing on the strategic who have missed the last step in painting tweaked job descriptions????. Help define new roles that drive more value. Do you choose to take ownership?

Recognize that all of these objectives will become a "want to" versus "have to" if you have purpose and have chosen to be the greatest in your chosen industry. This of course implies that you should stop comparing yourself to internal peers and how things used to be. Rather you should be focused on *what can be* to drive excellence in the broader peer group.

Also recognize that the exercises in this book are of equal value to other departments that tend to get sucked into day-to-day trench warfare. Some of these areas (i.e. administration, finance, facilities, HR, etc.) have similar challenges in keeping business purpose and strategy in focus. Take what you've learned and share your wisdom with them.

If you think there is something I should start, stop or think about doing to accomplish this mission better, send me an e-mail at craig@getoutofit.net. Although I have no expectation to gain great wealth or change the world with this book, I do hope to change your world. I hope that it can help get you and others to a better place. That is my purpose.

Author Biography

Craig Schiefelbein is the co-founder and CEO of Paragon Development Systems (PDS). PDS is an IT Services Company that has experienced 19 years of consecutive growth. PDS architects, supplies, implements and manages IT solutions for many fortune 500 companies.

Craig has directed aspects of PDS from innovation to market delivery. One of Craig's biggest "pride points" is that PDS has been recognized three times for building one of the "Best Places to Work" in Wisconsin.

Craig is the co-founder and chairman of the Oconomowoc Area Foundation. He serves as director for First bank Financial Center, College of Business and Economics; Innovation and Entrepreneurship UW Whitewater Advisory, Froedtert Hospitals President's Advisory Council, Specialized Marketing and various civic organizations.

Craig has been recognized as "Citizen of the Year" for his philanthropy and community service by the Chamber of Commerce. He has also been recognized as a finalist for Entrepreneur of the Year twice by Ernst and Young.

He and his wife, Mary, are the proud parents of three children, Hans, Klaus and Greta.

978-0-595-41357-7
0-595-41357-9

CPSIA information can be obtained at www.ICGtesting.com
Printed in the USA
BVOW031128281011

274697BV00001B/4/A

9 780595 413577